POLITICAL MONOPOLISTIC CAPITALISM

WEALTH CONCENTRATION SHEMA

UNITED STATES
TECONOMIC ANALYSIS
2014

Bahman Fakhraie, PhD

Copyright © Bahman Fakhraie PhD, 2012
All Rights Reserved
No Parts of this book shall be reproduced,
stored in retrieval systems, Or transmitted
by any means without written permission
from FERDAT Publishing, or
author, Dr. Bahman Fakhraie
ISBN-10:0989453995
ISBN-13:978-0-9894539-9-8
Library of Congress copyright
Case Number, 11156931041

POLITICAL MONOPOLISTIC CAPITALISM
&
WEALTH CONCENTRATION SCHEMA
UNITED STATES
TECONOMIC ANALYSIS,
2014

The Haves, The Have-Nothings, And The Have-Less

By

Bahman Fakhraie, PhD

2014

Acknowledgments

Many thanks, to family and friends. Bahman married Kay Davis 1976, master in Speech Pathology from Utah State University. His daughter, Lara Fatemeh Fakhraie, earned her Master's degree from Oregon State University. She is a published author. She resides in Oregon. His son, Anayat Fakhraie, a screenwriter earned his Master from the American Film Institute, and he is a member of WGAW. They did undergraduate work at University of Utah. Fakhraie families have endured revolutions, death of family, and hardships. The sui generis caravan of joy de vive continues. I wish for all of the family members, professors, teachers, students, helpers, and friends spread all over the globe my best wishes, warm thoughts, and many thanks. Life events are neither fair nor even. I wish you will learn from them, and they would always leave you better off than before.

Abstract

The book studies the millennial economic issues, which none-functionality and obstructionisms have accumulated nationally and internationally. Realistic educated new strategies out of the compound problems have evolved. These are productive functional methodologies toward improvements of the future economy. That makes 2014 year of functionality. Yet, the subject has lent it to demagogic populisms volatilities. Cautious and contemplative scholarship is respectfully required from all readers. The important gestalt of new technological injections and new variables of modular production processes are their applications in employment of all resources and not idleness of population, workers, graduates, and underpayment and reduction of money velocity of the macro economy towards functionality and fuller employment of constructive intends.

Contents

ACKNOWLEDGMENTS II
ABSTRACT III
LIST OF FIGURES VI
PREFACE VII
CHAPTER

1 POLITICAL MONOPOLISTIC CAPITALISM & WEALTH CONCENTRATION SCHEMA 1

    POLITICAL MONOPOLISTIC CAPITALISM & WEALTH CONCENTRATION SCHEMA 3
    MODERN PLIGHTS OF U-GRADUATES AND U-STUDENTS 4
    ARITHMETIC HOLISTIC VIEW 7
    HARSH HISTORIC ECONOMIC LIVES OF OTHERS 10
    NOTES 16

2 WEALTH-CONCENTRATION AND PERMANENT-WARS ECONOMIC SCHEMA 19

    WEALTH-CONCENTRATORS 21
    THE TECONOMETRICS 22
    JOB-CREATION 23
    GREAT LEADERSHIP 25
    NOTES 28

3 THE MISERLY PATH OF JOBLESS RECOVERY ... 29

    TINKLE-DOWN SPIN IS NOT MODERN ECONOMICS 43
    COOPERATE-CITIZENS' MINIMUM TAX LAW 45

ETHICAL AND MORAL COOPERATION, ETHICAL GOVERNMENTS 46

NOTES 51

4 A SHORT TERM ASSUMPTIVE 2014 FORECAST . 53

HOLISTIC PRODUCTIVE FUNCTIONALITY, FUTURE VISIONS 58

NOTES 65

APPENDIX 71

A ARITHMATIC OF OPTIMIZATION 72

B ARITHMATIC OF 74

ENTREPRENEURIAL TIME 74

C MAXIMIZATION OF GAINS, ... 76

OPTIMIZATION OF VALUE 76

D RATES OF GROWTH AND DECAY 82

FERDAT, AND LEGALS 83

SELECTED BIBLIOGRAPHY 97

CURRICULUM VITA 107

BOOK PROMOTIONS 115

List of Figures

Figure   Pages

1 Gross data by tax type fiscal years 1960–2010.. 30

2 Annual growth rate of USA population. 33

3, profits and wages as percentage of GDP. 36

4, Averages of USA employment growth rates. ... 39

5, Ten years averages of GDP growth rates......... 54

6, Growth rates of GDPUSA, 2008-2013 56

Preface

Dr. Bahman Fakhraie, PhD in economics, University of Utah, his dissertation added to the influences of the Unorthodox Holistic Economic doctrine and complemented the modern Orthodox economic theories, in the millennial age of technological paradigm shifts. He applies analytical skills with gestalt study of history, mathematics, and econometrics to economic analysis, with scientific background in his books. He is a published economist, author, researcher, investor, and private contractor. His skills are in international trade and finance, economic production (theory and application), growth and development theory, econometrics, agriculture economics, and agronomy.

The readers will note the organization of this book fallows table of content. This book is the result of many years of notes, journals, studies, learned skills, and exceptions to the rules, which Dr. Bahman Fakhraie wrote and accumulated at works and businesses, and complemented, by years of education since (1970s).

Dr. Bahman Fakhraie was invited by Senator Frank M. Browning to attend Utah State University, when Senator visited his family. After his master, he attended the University of Utah for the Ph.D. program in economics. He has met most of modern day science, business, and economic opinion leaders, and few other stars of their own fields. Dr. Bahman Fakhraie's book web page is at following link: http://bahfecon.wix.com/bahfecon.

CHAPTER 1

Political Monopolistic Capitalism & Wealth Concentration Schema

It will be difficult to discuss futuristic visions, which does not involve the plight of educators, students, and recent graduates, middle class, working (includes women heads of households) poor, and the poor children and elderly Americans. The international economic implications of these misalignments have been lived.[1] However, the effects are now pronounced and noticeable, morally by different religions, and ethically by different philosophies.

The demagogic history of the issues should not scare the reader away from an important discovery, that wealth creation element of free market, by job-creation and appropriate level of incomes in the relative free market mechanisms have been derailed by greed and self-indulgences.[2] The have been perverted away from the ethically accepted rules of capitalism in creation of decent jobs, livable salaries, sustainable functionalities system that feeds them too.

Despite the fact, that well enumerated inconsequential intellectuals are spinning mightily to present different Americans as the new welfare-queens of the moment, and create another victim subclass to demagogue on the 24/7 fake news-channels.

There are malfunctioned wealth concentration arrangements realigning the wealth creation mechanisms in the once functional capitalists' economies.[3] Since, this has been morphing over the last three decades the accumulated harm exceed the abilities of most small businesses to counter vial the currents.

The political monopolistic industrial organizations have mastered a self-destructive game, before they fully understand that they are its most likely victims, since they will have the most at risk. Therefore, they will have to finance most reparatory reworks. Therefore, cash-hoardings, minimum cooperate level tax avoidance are the wrong self-indulgences.

They know they are fulfilling a counter-productive duty to deflect and transpose the structurally widening real income gap in earnings and wealth concentration, and the breakdown of wealth creation in United States economy.

Political Monopolistic Capitalism & Wealth Concentration Schema

In fact, the unethical cacophony of monopolistic capitalism enslaved these once true representatives of this great exceptional American democratic republic so bad they readily overlooked, cooperate welfare queens, which are manipulating the social benefits and welfare system of the very poor to their underpaid-workers.

In face of historic profit, stock values, and CEO pay and bonus-checks, shamelessly, while they boldly under pay their taxes to refund the depleting reparatory systems. Those are the only reparatory systems available globally.

Modern Plights of U-graduates and U-students

In particular, I am very aware and sympathetic with the plight of modern university students, and recent graduate victims of the do-nothing political economic and great depression epoch, and the jobless recovery, two of their byproducts. I am glad some universities have discovered the plight of their long-suffering students now. Especially the ones that were bamboozled by a double whammy, the promised cheap student loan rates fixed at 3 percent, and then cheated by the ARM rate, that is now around 6-7 percent per annum.

The student walked into the post Iraq-war jobless-recovery economy, worsened by the obstructions of the wrong political party, austerity and sequestration, and their belated post-wars deficit hawking. Do you think those students will discover they are blocked out of casting their legal votes without reading? Voting rights are rescinded, blocked, reduced, and ham-hugged, in monopolistic one political party system at states levels.[4] There are valiant efforts by great lawmakers of both political parties.[5] Yet, this fast but not too deep mathematical study of comparative averages is not kind to the corporatist view, which tends to cheat the badly needed academic content-makers, modern innovators, and the middle class and working educators, and poor, which go under the budget buses readily.

The cooperation minimum tax, social security tax for higher incomes were not adopted, they were not even on the menu, but everyone else goring-oxen were on the menu. They want something for nothing for cooperate profit maximization, but they never want or understand the overall economic relative-competitive sustainability that maintains the balances, and encourages the circulatory conditions of demands and supplies.

The average tuition in some public university is estimated about $7000 per annum in 2013, in 1970s it was around $1000 a year. A book of about 200 pages or less was around $20 in 1970s. The arithmetic calculation of the relative ratios is solved by this kind of formulation, ($7000x$20)/$1000 = $140. That is the estimated average cost of the same kind of books in 2013 dollars. Most textbooks of less than 200 pages are priced at or around $80-$120 a book, if you look at your university bookstore.

Nevertheless, let us look at the bigger arithmetic picture. The economy that cheated the old students then, and plagiarized their works, subjected them to xenophobic bigotry, and under paid their wages then, now they may be the academics that are writing books. Because the same broken political machinery will accuse them of anger issues, greed, while cheating them out of good contracts, vanishing tenure systems, a livable level of living incomes and benefits, and let entropy eat out the infrastructural constructions beneath America.

Therefore, they will cheat the economy out of sustainable recoveries. Moreover, they will blame them for a decaying anachronistic criminal cooperate greed that aims and tends to rhetorical wealth-concentration, away from the wealth creation of modern teconomic sciences. That involves job-creation, too.

Arithmetic Holistic View

The bigger arithmetic pictures show the more holistic vision of these idiotic and reviled nightmares. Gasoline was $0.35 per gallon (in nominal terms), when I bought my first car, the blue jet, it is $3/gal, 2013. Now, that is 857 percent increase for the last 35 years, 22 percent a year.

Average U-CEO (a U. administer) salary was $100,000. It is about $1 million now. That is at the poor house-Us, state public universities. That is 1000 percent increase, 28.6 percent per annum.

The costs of cable connected big screen TV is $1000+$2400 is equal to $3400 per year. The cost of the TV was $200 the rest was free, 1975. That is 1700 percent cost of living adjustment. It is 48.6 percent per year. I will not further elucidate cooperate CEOs 500 plus times over the Americans' average incomes of $40,000 a year. However, let us face it. The $40,000 seems two times higher than most average salaries around your neighborhoods.

The Sponged-brain damaged sportsmen on the cable sport channels 24/7, some are sometime lucky in the shorter run. Only those lucky few will get million dollars contracts, and the unlucky many will parish in solitudes with damaged brains and mostly penniless.[6] That is the human savagery of the last two millenniums, which continues unabated. It is one of most intellectually dishonest human right abuses for cooperate entertainments of our lifetimes, since the fall of blasted gladiators of Roma. Children, university players, and pros are all subjects of cooperate brain-sponge-making money-machine for profit.[7] Yet, corporatist anti-educators will want to add the academic book writers to the bodies of these victims.

Things will really get ugly, if we raise the curtain and look under the table of the bombastic anger mongers, and bloviating blow hearts of modern cable-media. You know the $10 & $11 million dollars a year nabobs of negativities, and the 24/7 nothingness, the true masters of blubbering mental incertitude, and the squeaking windmills of their minds. The same corporatist-blue-dogs and their corporatist' charlatans that declared class warfare on the middle class, working poor, graduates, and absolute poor some 30 years ago, they are still at it, again. Trickle-down doubtful economic assertions became tinkle-down political spins a long time ago. The war on intellectuals and academic started with Nixon, not yesterday by a few rightwing nuts.

Teachers have been bamboozled like everyone else, with almost all of the middle class workers for a flat 2-4 percent per year cost of living adjustment, while the rest of economy has been pulling ahead, which is causing the slow recovery. I think cheating your academics, or book writers out of their share will damage you where it really hurts, in your personal economy, aside from their rights to exercise of their legal options and remedies. You can always stay in the ocean of ignorance and 'curse the recondite darkness'. The obsolete cooperation spinners hope you will be used to it, and become their cooperation intellectual and eye slaves. I suggest you read the good books, even if it financially helps the intellectuals and the academics sometimes.

<u>Harsh Historic Economic Lives of Others</u>

The Great Millennial Legacy of Nelson Mandela (1918-2013) is a shared experience with other leaders of the civil right and nonviolent movement internationally.

The three continents none-violent political and economic movements advanced and learned from the life story of Madiba in the last two millenniums. The great legacy of President Nelson Mandela contains many accomplishments. He was the modern leader of the nonviolent political movement for freedom, justice, and an egalitarian, peaceful, and finally and mostly productive co-existence political movement. He was also a freedom fighter, announced and denounced, and jailed terrorist, and finally the universally admired President of South Africa.

President Mandela shared his beloved country and Africa with India's Mohandas Mahatma Gandhi.[8] Their timelines and shared life story are amazingly similar.[9] Gandhi, Mandela, together with Dr. Martin Luther king Jr. they gifted three continents, of America, Africa, and Asia with the freedom, peace, and justice and the successful nonviolent co-existence.[10] These multicultural political civil right movements advanced humanitarian lives and the personal economies of all races on three continents.

The reviviscences of great human persons of last and this millennial history is a severe but required admonition of the long gallops away from democratic and constitutional jurisprudence, into the hate-lands of state militaristic-intrusions, or technology-intensive violence against privacy and property of citizens with massive collateral damages. States can fool the citizenry with false security, while they abolish their rights and humanities. The old media documented the three vanquished harangues in history extensively, if the commercial modern media wanted to do reality-exposition of facts of history.

The life and time of Mahatma Gandhi evolved from overt violence of South African Apartheid, mono-racial domination politics, to then India, under colonial economic domination of overt racial-politics.

These governments were using technological advancements of their times, not for economic advancements of their population, or the majority of their population, but for domination, political and economic objectification, and control of the majority of their populations, which happened to be black and brown. Utilizing technologies as paper please laws, individual monitoring for control. They would have immediately adopted E-verify, Cell phone tapping, computer implants, if they had the technology. They would have applied them for the profiling and subjugation rather than advancement of their population.

The moral of stories of lives and times of Mohandas Mahatma Gandhi, Dr. Martin Luther King Jr., and President Nelson Mandela are not the success or the whitewash of state terrorisms as public control policies.

Since, the states would use jails, guns, bullets, and advanced technologies (drones & robotics), and violent terminations of privacies, and human dignities, against their population. It is the success and advancement of human causes of even marginalized people, their freedom, one-person one vote, economic and political rights, triumphs of justice, dignity of making a living, jobs, and working within humanitarian frameworks and laws.

The exclusionary politics and policies they fought, and the 'inclusion' of politics and economics they advanced, all benefited more people. They employed more than one race or group economically. Some of the basic facts escaped then the President Ronald Regan administration, but not both houses of representatives, when they overturned the President Ronald Reagans White House veto on divestments from Apartheid-government of South Africa, (as W.H. shared sympathy with Europe, Israel, and some other nations).

We would all live smaller economic lives, if we forget their lives-lessons from their lifelong struggles internationally. It is astonishing how easily these lessons are lost on big and small, democratic or dictatorial modern governments. Perhaps great gatherings of leaders in his great memory will advance greater causes of peace, egalitarian job-income equities, more trades, and more job-creations.

Notes

[1] "The 85 richest people on Earth now have the same amount of wealth as the bottom half of the global population, the Oxfam report says."
Jim Puzzanghera, Oxfam report highlights widening income gap between rich, poor, *Los Angeles Times*, 4:45 PM PST, January 20, 2014,
http://www.latimes.com/business/la-fi-income-inequality-20140121,3318931,331291,print.story.
And, (Inequality has shot up the global agenda in recent years: US President Obama has made it a key priority for 2014. The World Economic Forum (WEF) has identified widening income disparities as the second greatest worldwide risk in the next 12-18 months. WEF's Global Outlook report, published in November, warned inequality is undermining social stability and 'threatening security on a global scale.'),
Winnie Byanyima, Wealth of half the world's population now the same as that of tiny elite, *Executive Director, Oxfam International*, Published: 20 January 2014,
http://www.oxfam.org/en/pressroom/pressrelease/2014-01-20/rigged-rules-mean-economic-growth-increasingly-winner-takes-all-for-rich-elites
Oxfam report 13,
http://www.oxfam.org/sites/www.oxfam.org/files/oxfam-annual-report-2012-2013.pdf

[2] Philip Pullella, Pope attacks global economics for worshipping 'god of money', CAGLIARI, Sardinia (Reuters), September 22, 2013, and
KATIE MCDONOUGH, Pope condemns economic inequality while the Vatican continues to censure nuns' anti-poverty work, Salon, MONDAY, SEP 23, 2013 10:35 AM MDT

[3] Sargent Shriver and peace corps efforts, http://www.sargentshriver.org/gallery/the-peace-corps http://www.cnn.com/2014/01/08/politics/war-on-poverty-50-years/index.html?utm_source=feedburner&utm_medium=feed&utm_campaign=Feed%3A+rss%2Fcnn_allpolitics+%28RSS%3A+Politics%29.

[4] Sari Horwitz, Pennsylvania judge strikes down voter ID law, *the Washington post*, http://www.washingtonpost.com/world/national-security/pennsylvania-judge-strikes-down-voter-id-law/2014/01/17/472d620e-7fa2-11e3-93c1-0e888170b723_story.html

[5] Lawmakers Roll Out Voting Rights Act Fix CARRIE JOHNSON, Lawmakers Roll Out Voting Rights Act Fix, NPR, January 16, 2014 3:52 PM, http://www.npr.org/blogs/itsallpolitics/2014/01/16/263113258/lawmakers-roll-out-voting-rights-act-fix

[6] Hal Hodson, Brain damage in American football linked to head trauma, *Newscientist*, 15:04 17 October 2013, http://www.newscientist.com/article/dn24420-brain-damage-in-american-football-linked-to-head-trauma.html

[7] Sara Ganim, CNN analysis: Some college athletes play like adults, read like 5th-graders, CNN, updated 1:05 PM EST, Wed January 8, 2014, http://www.cnn.com/2014/01/07/us/ncaa-athletes-reading-scores/index.html#

[8] Mohandas Gandhi (1869-1948) - Columbia University, http://www.columbia.edu/cu/weai/exeas/asian-revolutions/pdf/gandhi-timeline.pdf

[9] Gandhi in South Africa, Key events during Mahatma Gandhi's 21 years in South Africa,theguardian.com, Wednesday 29 July 2009 14.43 EDT, http://www.theguardian.com/world/2009/jul/29/gandhi-south-africa-timeline

[10] "The keynote speaker will be Arun Gandhi, grandson of the Indian civil rights leader.
"Jesus gave me the message, Gandhi gave me the method," Sid Gates quoted King as saying." And
Arun Gandhi experienced discrimination himself as a child in South Africa by both whites, who thought he was "too black," and blacks who thought he was "too white," according to his Web site."
Lisa Kaylor, Gandhi's grandson to speak at MLK event, Friday, Jan. 10, 2014,
http://chronicle.augusta.com/life/your-faith/2014-01-10/gandhis-grandson-speak-mlk-event

CHAPTER 2

Wealth-Concentration and Permanent-Wars Economic Schema

Blame anything for the jobless economic recovery, but the bad policies that caused it. If you do not fully comprehend the powers of imperfect competition and the full implication of organization power in keeping wages low and disposable income flat for three decade, you will go blame something else (it can be technologies) for economic joblessness, you blame everything you do not understand.

Paddling plumping jobs, low wage jobs, and two-year college degrees when you have substantially kept DPI low, is a new intellectual lowbrow politics, slithers out of the failed supply-siders and our friends in that desperate political party, and their embedded journalistic companions, which deported the middle class job creators and jail-warehouses the unemployed youth and minorities.

However, they have clung to that new economic religion as readily as blame guns, or technology as if these entities can think and do thing for themselves, and they can dispossess massive populations, or keep wages and incomes increases flat as a percentage of GDP, for the middle class, labors, workers, graduates, since 1970s.

Perhaps, next we will hear that it is the technology that is pumping cooperate citizens (the other new entities') money into local, national, and presidential campaigns, for certain laws, while suppresses the voters rights, and fight reasonable health care for all citizen, or a functional comprehensive immigration bill. They will not represent efficiently, the majorities that are portrait as takers.

Yet, the do-nothing-congress persons still are paid, and they receive their universal healthcare, while they are not doing the citizens business.

Wealth-Concentrators

Wealth-Concentrators They sing free-enterprise economy, but they do not see anything wrong with massive shoveling of money, 500 time more than average incomes to one class as CEO wages. If you do not want to pay your taxes on that ill-gotten public money in your own private catchy, of course you will blame anything or anyone to disguise the facts. Therefore, instead of pushing for a functional constitutional democracy, more balanced sustainable fiscal policies, and monetary policies, you blame inanimate objects for wrecking the middle class economic conditions. Instead of cost of living raises, level of living wages for educators, workers, you blame them for what your underfunding urban and rural education has caused.

They pay for hack journalism, and backward embedded journalism, small-minded scholarship, and fake wars, which kill and dispose real people. I think American citizens already know who will wreck USA economy, because they are the same people who already wrecked the middle class USA, Detroit, Stockton, others. The American and people globally know it was not an IT.

The Teconometrics

It was not elderly measly pension fund contracts. The investor bankers, their political industrial complex, deregulated the laws and swindled them out of their IRA, stock funds, and pension benefits, and usurious student loans, and no-jobs recoveries, well before the new crew shown up for their shameful legacy banners.

Econometrics Relation of Employment and Disposable Personal Income Data

> Av rg tot 7.2 slope of job/dspi 1959-2013
> 0.150135321
> Av rg 3.66 slope of job/dspi 2003-2013
> 0.051169688
> RSQ tot 1959-2013 0.871441531
> Corr tot 1959-2013 0.933510327

Natural logarithm growth rates, and averages, and slope regression and RSQ, and Corr for correlation among employment and disposable personal income indices are used.

Beyond positive correlation, there is the magnitude of slopes. That is much higher for total data 1959-2013, monthly data of dpi, and total employment, when average growth rate of dpi was higher at 7.2 percent 1959-2013, versus the average growth rate of 3.66 percent for 2003-2013. That is also reconfirmed, by a positive relation and correlation 93 percent, and total data shown by RSQ 0.87 for total data 1959-2013. Some summation can note the higher growth rate 3-7 with much higher job growth slope. That overall job-creation performance was 3 time higher than the millennial recovery periods of job creation from the year 2003 to year 2013.

Job-Creation

Despite Jeers or Adulation, Job-Creation We Must! (9-20-2011). Europeans' political fascinations with extreme right, even after messianic terrorisms by far right individuals, are cause for further contemplations. One prepends, is it rumination for economic enlightenments, or the unfortunate regurgitation of past nightmares. The suppositions, which blame multiculturalism (mostly Moslem emigrants this time, it was Jews a few generation back), in otherwise exclusionary and elitists' cultures, neither contributes or assists Islamic scholars in moderation of Islamic radicalism, nor can it curb the implosive peculations, which have increased joblessness and multicultural misfortunes equally.

They have the immorality of latent Machiavellianism, and the violence of Uncle Adolf's Menageries; nevertheless, they have no remedies for mass reemployment.

European governments chose expensive and failed but essential macroeconomic experimentalisms and joblessness, which encouraged the far rights' erroneous trite suppositions.

Great Leadership

Leaderships that fear the extreme right will again fail the Western world. In time of economic scarcities, which will test or prohibit "beg thy neighbors" dependencies, leadership is needed. Will the great leadership prevail?

Thus, financing adventurousness without full benefit of free trades and enhanced commercial-international trades (otherwise, healthy economies) will only serve as determents to free commerce. These situations will only encourage prudence of diplomacy over carte blanche (blank checks) militarisms. Historically, this modesty of intend seem to have been imposed on the leaderships repeatedly. Even United State will have hard enough time, to shift from war footing into domestic economically enhanced job-creations.

It is amazing how imperceptibly, with a short skip from the haloed high halls of higher education to certain political catacombs Job-creationism retrogrades into theological creationism; alas, the echoes are trite, untrue, unconvincing, and displaced logical constructions and maintenances of sounders structures, and hypothesis, all available to functional democratic free market economies.

Deregulations can be more harmful than bad regulation. Deregulation of meat industry can lead to bacterial outbreaks. Deregulation of clean-coal industries can give us cave-ins in our numerous global coalmines and string of death, toxic streams and lake, acid rain, and the same old expedited carbon-over-loads.[1] Relaxed regulation can unchain petroleum deep-water cowboy-drillings, which wasted Southeast food industry, and for years and billions of dollars, yet to be fully and economically studied.

The unhindered nuclear energy industries can shut down and radiate a third to half of another nation for years and trillion dollars, yet to be partially comprehended or researched.[2] The unencumbered natural gas industries can proceed with their deep well fracturing, yet to be economically researched, or fully disclosed, which can duplicate the deep well spill disaster on land. Currently, we have to take the words of the industry in forms of commercial outtakes for the future of this great nation.

Deregulation of investment banking, the cowboy-securitization of mortgage-industries without the jeered consumer protection regulations, and the fought-regulations of derivative industries have done more than BenLadenism did, but they do it internally. Mr. Madoff goes without roommates and poker hands, awaiting many global political and financial mega-Madoffs.[3] The justice department can barely keep up with them.[4] Yet, no one is droned Wall Street shenanigans, or all of these white-color crimes in USA, or Europe.

Notes

[1] Alexandra Field. Meridith Edwards and Catherine E. Shoichet, West Virginia chemical spill shines spotlight on loose regulation, *CNN,* updated 10:39 PM EST, Mon January 13, 2014http://www.cnn.com/2014/01/13/us/west-virigina-chemical-contamination/

[2] Dr. Bahman Fakhraie, Teconomics of Dynamic Risks, http://www.amazon.com/Teconomics-oF-Dynamic-Risks-ebook/dp/B00CUNPJZ6/ref=sr_1_1?s=digital-text&ie=UTF8&qid=1368893440&sr=1-1&keywords=Dr+bahman+fakhraie

[3] Nate Raymond, Judge criticizes lack of prosecution against Wall Street executives for fraud, Reuters, NEW YORK Tue Nov 12, 2013 7:10pm EST, http://www.reuters.com/article/2013/11/13/financial-judge-idUSL2N0IX1B620131113

[4] Cary O'Reilly and Linda Sandler, Judges Punish Wall Street as Regulators Just Talk About Reform, *Bloomberg,* September 8, 2009 00:01 EDT http://www.bloomberg.com/apps/news?pid=newsarchive&sid=a5wZ95KdSuJQ

CHAPTER 3

The Miserly Path of Jobless Recovery

Therefore, the suppositions of the executive suites and their paid lobbyists, that it is either Dodge City or full-unemployment, are manufactured manageress of dangerously unpatriotic greedy war-robots.

The sententious absolutisms seeds to encumber job-creation for political misdeed will yield unfortunate shared harvests. It will only add to the other sins of union bashing, low-wage control, discernible capital mobility, defalcation of national wealth in the recent path for permanent-wars, and dishonest upward wealth-concentrations.

It will add to the perceptual sins of domestic populism for greed and self-enrichments without the promised shared social benefits. Figure 1 shows the gap between individual income taxes, and business taxes.[1]

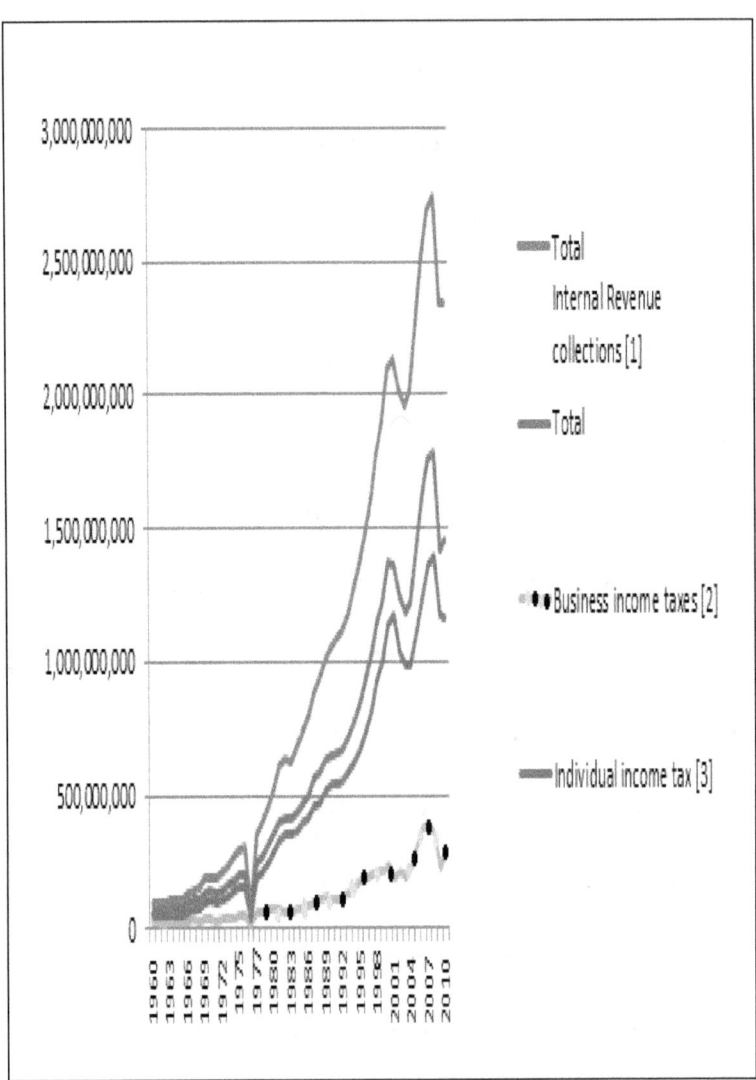

Figure 1, Gross data, by tax type, Fiscal Years 1960–2010
Note.
http://www.irs.gov/taxstats/article/0,,id=171960,00.html
Calculation and graph by author.

The econometrical analysis of the magnitude of slope of growth rates, show three important points.

$\partial T \partial It \geq \Omega 1$

$\partial T \partial Bt \geq \Omega 2$

One is the positive direction of increases. However, what is alarming, is not only the difference, largeness of omega one, over omega two, but the rate of taxation in omega one. It shows that more is extorted than received by individuals under the current system. That is what has been unsustainable for some time.

$\Omega 1 \approx 1.02$

$\Omega 2 \approx 0.77$

Therefore, the cogent solutions incognizance in these complex arithmetic of taxation rate analysis of statistical slope of growth rate of actual collection from different classifications by IRS are also yield adventitious answers.

Unfortunately, for the nescience political party, increasing fees and further taxes on the larger omega will prove counterproductive. Job-creation will increase the base, but the quality of the jobs, and take home real income is the determinant policy jolt.

Unfortunately, for the nescience political party, increasing fees and further taxes on the larger sigma will prove counterproductive. Job-creation will increase the base, but the quality of the jobs, and take home income is the determinant policy jolt.

Especially, it becomes hypocritical, when they have deemed the lower sigma a job killer repeatedly. That is why the insistence that immigration law modification had been urged incessantly away from the populous emotionalism nature of the 1996 alteration to that law. Because simply halving sigma one will not be accomplished by nativist sentimentality. That is even after full employment policy implementation of government job for all PhDs including, liberal arts graduates. Figure 2 shows the annual growth rate of USA population.

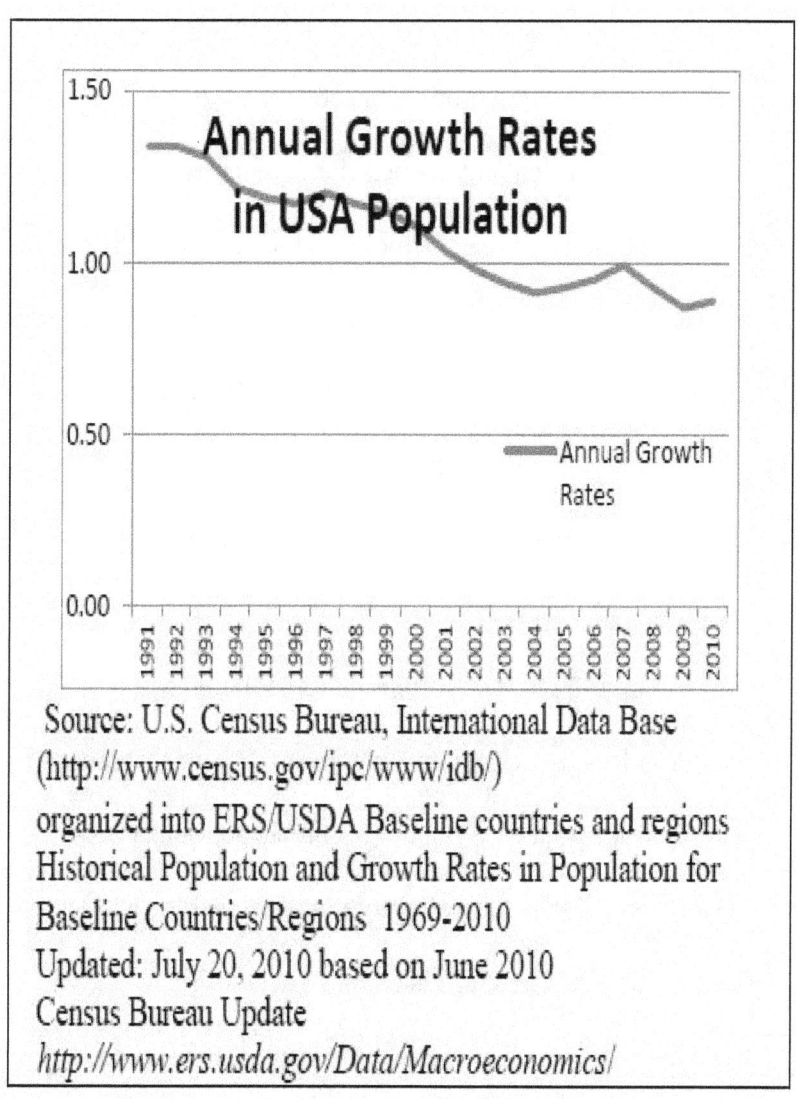

Figure 2 Annual growth rate of USA population.

The dynamic nature of population decline and the baby-boomers population-spikes are dynamic econometrics' composition certainties. Moreover, the CEO wages, bonuses, and looting fiascos are simply not sufficient to widen and deepen the base revenues.

There have been some Ponzi schemes and some Al Capone angles, and now we find out they will not even pay their fair tax shares to fix the country, which they get to enjoy more comparatively.

The lowest green graph shows how much the business paid versus the individual income taxes, total income taxes paid, and total revenue collated by IRS. Nevertheless, American middle class, elderlies, students and their mega student loans ($30 to $300 thousands), academics, teachers, firefighters, policepersons, and legal immigrants are the victims of these destabilizing peculations, as the political onionskins peel off these rotting-political party two-step shuffles.

Americans are discovering the real perpetrators of the heinous unpatriotic greed and cash-hording for the new millennium, the patriot acts I, II, FISA laws were not for them or their security.

They live on the hill, and they do not want to pay their fair share of taxes, which maintains the colored glassed cathedrals on those hills. Worst yet, they ignore sage consul. The few percentage adjustment in the mega billions will not harm but benefit the country, and the economy, if it goes toward true job-creation, and by money-velocity and commerce will come back in your tills, after the multiple sometimes global circulations.

It is an astonishment that this known abstract hypothesis escape leaders of industry and political hacks alike, easily. Since, it encroaches on their monopolistic cooperate share of national wealth, incrementally. Hence, they are the makers, and all other people are the takers. Figure 3 shows profits and wages as percentage of GDP.

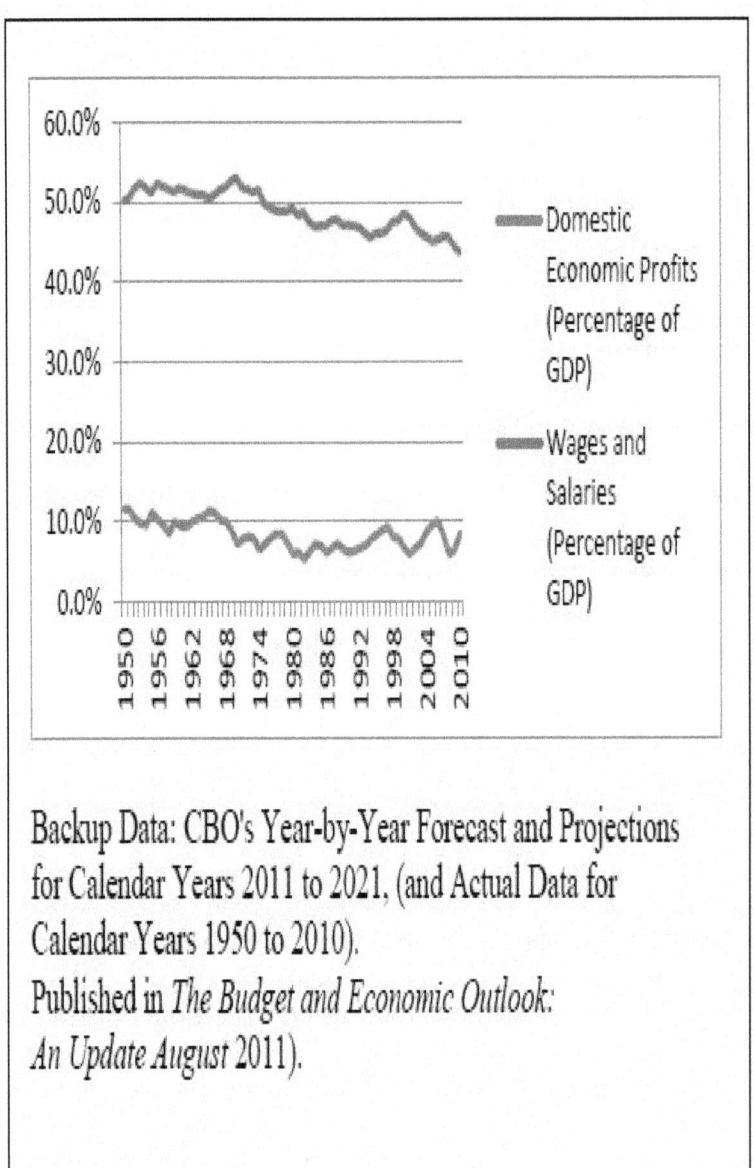

Figure 3, profits and wages as percentage of GDP.

Since 1970s, the declines in growth rate of population and wages, and profit as percent of economy are prominent. Moreover, math will tell us the 10 percent of the economy alone cannot master job-creation that the 55 percent of the economy did in the good old days, government is part of this deductive job-creation solution. However, paying their share is a good start.

This would have been much easier, if demand side technological injections were much larger and were aimed at domestic nondefense expansions, it went to tarp one (the save the investment bankers fund, the American version, and then the European version), and over the table defense and under the table defense, the mushrooming and unaccountable security concrete. So, we do not know other than the few people that touch your junks in airport, are there job-creations or criminal frauds under the security acts, or cash transfers in airports of Baghdad and Kabul? Even thou, they claim they did not see more than 2 or 3 million dollars in roads and buildings in these countries! However, certain political party has had ample times to play abstractionisms, abandonments, denial and blame, catcalls and jeers, along with their new "do-nothing religion absolutions."

Therefore, we are supposed to shut off the 2.5 million-government job engines meekly in a bad prolonged recession, while cooperation hoarded profits and cash, and discernibly lumbered 1.5 million temp-type work and Mac-jobs, excluding the executive bonus bundles. All these time small businesses were snookered out of capital market, and the middle class are bamboozled out of the payroll tax breaks to boost aggregate demand temporarily. Remember that social security number check President Bush sent you 2001, that is that peak in 2002-2003 in the above graph. Why are they squabbling about another boost to the middle-class? Figure 4 show the average growth rates of USA employment.

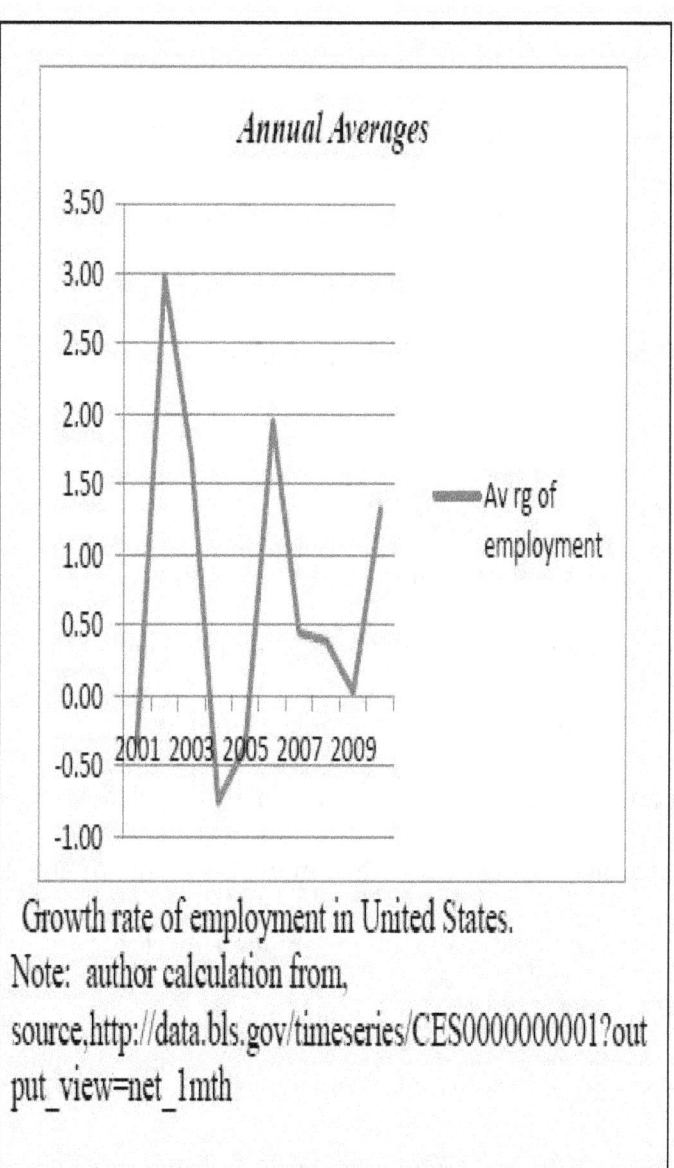

Growth rate of employment in United States.
Note: author calculation from,
source,http://data.bls.gov/timeseries/CES0000000001?output_view=net_1mth

Figure 4, Averages of USA employment growth rates.

Why are they hauling deficit. This latent riotousness of reformed perennial deficit-spending sinners is cheap political theater for their well-coddled meal tickets and your passive votes.

Hence, we start over with another true job-creation plan amongst the jeers, instead of adulations. We have more economic tools to deal with inflations, but sparse few tools to deal with stagflations.

The American infrastructures, unlike the mushrooming security buildings, are fading away in neglect, pancaking roads and bridges, imploding-waterways undergrounds, and the disemboweled schools. These entire infrastructure and more, the employment of teachers and professors, they want the America to languish with quotidian joblessness, while they amass thirty more silver and gold coins! Here are domestic wolves and BenLadenism we can no longer effort. Moreover, the hypocrisy and the unintellectual contortions are painful to all constituencies, which suffer from the negligence of these parties "irreligious absolutions."

American people as people around the globe have too many shared lives, their familial, friendly and commerce connections to succumb to depression of efforts and smallness of bad intentions, and illiberal narrowness of mind. That is, that didactic poetry the madness of far rights cannot comprehend about legal immigration, about freedom that all people seek. The scientific wholeness and modernity of positivism seeded in the modern functional communities, which multiculturalism has cultivated even outside academic high halls.

People will know, not to trust the same power drunk, tax the poor and middle class crews, with their economic lives, again. Not unless, they are sure, they are well away from the depression ledges, that the political party led them there, and left them there, not long ago. You ought not to be able to fool all of the people, all of time. It is unnatural, and yes counter intellectual, unscientific, even illiberal. We sure have not seen signs of intellectual economic lives among the other political party, despite the full-time alien probing

Especially, it becomes hypocritical, when they have deemed the lower omega as a job killer repeatedly. That is why the insistence that immigration law modification had been urged incessantly away from the emotionalism nature of the 1996 alterations to that law. The attainment of omega-one will not be accomplished by nativist sentimentality. That is even after full employment policy implementation of government job for all PhDs including, liberal arts graduates.

The dynamic nature of population decline and the baby-boomers population-spikes are dynamic econometrics' composition certainties. Moreover, the CEO wages, bonuses, and looting fiascos are simply not sufficient to widen and deepen the base revenues, and government revenues to do the jobs.

Tinkle-Down Spin Is Not Modern Economics

There have been some Ponzi schemes and some Al Capone angles, and now we find out they will not even pay their fair tax shares to fix the country. Nevertheless, American middle class, elderlies, students and their mega student loans ($30 to $300 thousands), academics, teachers, firefighters, policepersons, and legal immigrants are the victims of these destabilizing peculations, as the political onionskins peel off these rotting-political party two-step shuffles.

However, the monopolistic political advocacies take own the system, wash out monopoly taxation, reline them on the lower incomes, adjust the revenue and protect the cooperate welfare and spin it for the constituencies.

Americans are discovering the real perpetrators of the heinous unpatriotic greed and cash-hording for the new millennium, the PATRIOT Acts I, II, FISA laws were not for their securities. The golden goose laid the golden eggs for the insider of the security-military industrial complex.[2] It was to pilfer business strategies, private records, phone calls and e-mails illegally, retrenchment of global commerce and global backlash are the accumulated results.[3] The international security and cooperation have retrenched.[4] Thus, they have opened business fields for the competition to flourish.

They live on the hills, high on the hogs, and they do not want to pay their fair share of taxes, which maintains the colored-glassed cathedrals on those higher hills. Worst yet, they ignore sage consul. The few percentage adjustment in your mega billions will not harm but benefit the country, and the economy, if it goes toward true job-creation, instead of miserly political jobs, or crony security-job creationism and in-house featherbeddings.

Since 1970s, the declines in growth rate of population and wages, and profit as percent of economy are prominent. Moreover, math will tell us the 1 percent or even the 10 percent of the economy alone cannot master job-creation that the 55 percent of the economy did in the good old days, government is part of this deductive job-creation solution.

Cooperate-Citizens' Minimum Tax Law

However, paying their share is a good start. This would have been much easier, if demand side technological injections were much larger and were aimed at domestic nondefense expansions, it went to tarp one (the save the investment bankers fund, the American version, and then the European version), and over the table defense and under the table defense, the mushrooming and unaccountable security concretes. So, we do not know other than the few people that touch your junks in airport, are there job-creations or criminal frauds under the security acts, or cash transfers in airports of Baghdad and Kabul? Even thou, these country claim they did not see more than 2 or 3 million dollars in roads and buildings in these countries, while American taxpayers are billed for 4-trillion dollars permanent wars!

However, certain political party has had ample times to play abstractionisms, abandonments, denial and blame, catcalls and jeers, along with their new "do-nothing religion absolutions."

Ethical and moral Cooperation, Ethical Governments

Therefore, we are supposed to shut off the 2.5 million-government job engines meekly in a bad prolonged recession in economic-lifesaving sequestrations and austerity plans.

Therefore, underfunding infrastructure rebuilding and national investments are disruptive to employments. While cooperation strategists have hoarded profits and cash, and discernibly lumbered 1.5 million temp-type work and Mac-jobs, excluding the executive bonus bundles, cash bundles offshores, thus reducing the multiplier effect. In the meantime, the political monopolistic cooperate machinery applies reelection-funds and law making organization power of political monopoly to reduce their taxes and government revenues. Therefore, they are shutting down the fiscal job-creation systems.

All these time small businesses were snookered out of capital market, and the middle class are bamboozled out of the payroll tax breaks, which boosted aggregate demand temporarily. In addition, the immigrant job-creators are jailed and deported systematically, with Machiavellian law manipulations, legalese, and disruptive none-functionalities.

United States job creation machine is still not making enough jobs to maintain employment levels positive. Remember that social security number check President Bush sent you 2001, that is that peak in 2002-

2003 economy. Why are they squabbling about any boost to the middle-class, or job creation investments? Why are they hollering deficit at 7 to 25 percent unemployed of minorities, women, and older workers. This latent riotousness of reformed perennial deficit-spending sinners is cheap political theater for their well-coddled meal tickets and your votes 2014 and 2016.

Therefore, ethical and moral cooperation and businesses, ethical governments will be a new good starts toward the national and global improvements summit.

Hence, we start over with another true job-creation plan amongst the jeers, instead of adulations. We have more economic tools to deal with inflations, but sparse few tools to deal with stagflations. The American infrastructures, unlike the mushrooming security buildings, are fading away in neglect, pancaking roads and bridges, imploding-waterways undergrounds, and the disemboweled and closed schools.

These entire infrastructure and more, the employment of teachers and professors, they want the America to languish with quotidian joblessness, while they amass thirty more silver and gold coins! Here are domestic wolves and BenLadenism we can no longer effort. So, why do we vote them back in habitually, instead of weeding them out intellectually. Moreover, the hypocrisy and the unintellectual contortions are painful to all constituencies, which suffer from the negligence of these parties "irreligious absolutions." American people as people around the globe have too many shared lives, their familial, friendly and commerce connections to succumb to depression of efforts and smallness of bad intentions, and illiberal narrowness of mind, and multibillion dollars permanent war mongering machines.

That is, that didactic poetry, which the madness of far rights cannot comprehend about legal immigration, about freedom that all people seek, and exuberance that it injects in the job creation machinery of modern economies.[5] The scientific wholeness and modernity of positivism seeded in the modern functional communities, which multiculturalism has cultivated even outside academic high halls, among clergies, business people, and job-creating communities with positive attitude about their futures.

Notes

[1] http://www.irs.gov/taxstats/article/0,,id=171960,00.html

[2] "If House bill 2272 became law, the state of Washington would not cooperate with federal agencies in any warrantless electronic surveillance. Called the Fourth Amendment Protection Act, the bill would establish a state policy to refuse participation in electronic data collection on any person without a warrant and would make it a misdemeanor for state officials to do so. Rep. David Taylor, R-Moxee, is sponsoring the bill.
"It seemed like every single day there was an article about NSA (National Security Agency) surveillance," Taylor said. "We thought if the federal government is going to refuse to address the issue, that's what the state will aim for."), Posted by Ashley Stewart, Bill would prohibit state from cooperating in warrantless electronic surveillance, January 17, 2014 at 2:44 PM, http://blogs.seattletimes.com/politicsnorthwest/2014/01/17/bill-would-prohibit-state-from-cooperating-in-warrantless-electronic-surveillance/

[3] Wieland Wagner, Brand Expansion, China's Race to Conquer World Markets, Spiegel, 01/08/2014 04:38 PM, http://www.spiegel.de/international/business/chinese-brands-expanding-into-world-markets-a-942094-druck.html

[4] "NSA and GCHQ operations have shaken trust between countries that considered themselves allies, the report says." Nick Hopkins and Ian Traynor, NSA and GCHQ activities appear illegal, says EU parliamentary inquiry, Civil liberties committee report demands end to

indiscriminate collection of personal data by British and US agencies, *The Guardian*, Thursday 9 Jan., 2014, 12.02 EST, http://www.theguardian.com/world/2014/jan/09/nsa-gchq-illegal-european-parliamentary-inquiry

[5] James Barragan, Immigration reform must be top priority, Commerce secretary says, *Los Angeles Times*, January 9, 2014, 6:00 p.m.
http://www.latimes.com/business/money/la-fi-mo-immigration-reform-us-commerce-secretary-20140109,0,3742150.story#ixzz2qhpY1prn,

CHAPTER 4

A Short Term Assumptive 2014 Forecast

It is important to look at the caliber of economic challenges, before setting or reassessing the economic journey ahead. The greedy intentions and miserliness of purposes have failed us measurably. The one percent upper income levels may have miscalculated the size and the impacts of the downsides, which would affect their interests that is above 80 percent, versus the 20 percent or less of accumulations of all others in this modern economy.

In those scholarly endeavors at macroeconomics and strategic levels, comparative studies of indices lends a valuable helping hand, to the educated-minds' eyes. Figure 5 studies the annual rate of growth calculated by the logarithmic formulations. It shows a dismaying trend line for most of this millennium.

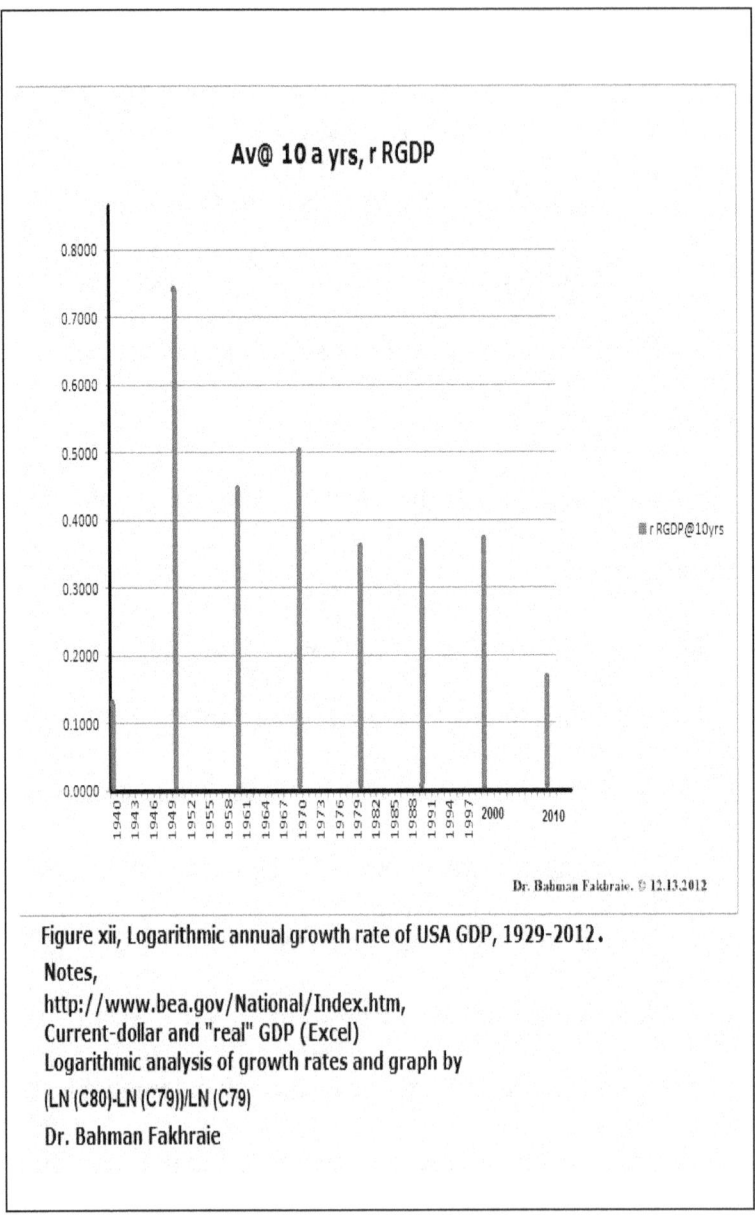

Figure 5, Ten years averages of GDP growth rates.

It is a dismaying index, because it is the ten-year averages of growth rates of real Gross domestic product of United States declining since 1970s. Rates of population decay, percentage of wage and profits from GDP dropping, declining averages rate of employment are indices with important forces, unless a true recovery is replacing the false jobless recoveries of the recent past.

Figure 6 improves the odds by studying the antithetical proposition despite the size of the recovery and the miserliness of governmental investments in the economy. There are positive indications of small upticks in the trend line in recent data. Assuming that holds, the forecast can improve.

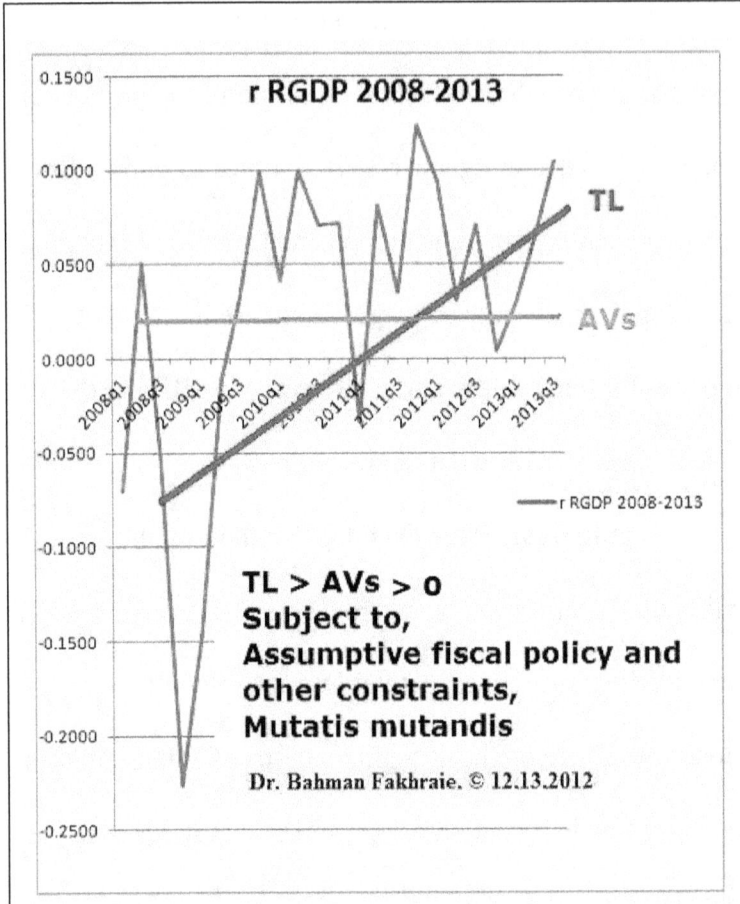

Figure 6, Growth rates of GDP-USA, 2008-2013

Nevertheless, onslaught of political mischiefs, austerity and sequestration schema, incompetence in job creation strategies, shutdown fevers, are numbers of ill winds that may not relent. Yet there is that good news forecasts for the New Year 2014, given the functionality assumptions hold, mutatis mutandis.

Given, TL > AVs > 0

The forecasts are subject to, assumptive fiscal policy, organizational strains of imperfect competition from duopolistic to monopolistic modus operandi, and other political constraints functionality versus games-returns expectations, Mutatis mutandis.

This is a limited forecast, but it sets the logarithmic growth rate of chained-gross domestic product north of 2.4 to < 6.4, distributive rebalance, reasonable jobs, and value-exchange theories (livable wages) are also part of the nationally refocused economic scene. That will prove the engine of growth for the global economy, if peaceful diplomacy averts pitfalls induced or caused for the usual political suspects.

Hence, the short-term trend line chained Gross Domestic Product (RGDP) is larger than the averages growth rate of GDP, and they are both greater than zero and positive, the probability improves toward a positive trend in a growing economy subjects to the assumptive conditions imposed.

Holistic Productive Functionality, Future Visions

People will know, not to trust the same power drunk, tax the poor and middle class crews, with their economic lives, again. Not unless, they are sure, they are well away from the depression ledges, that the political party led them there, and left them there, not long ago. You ought not to be able to fool all of the people, all of time. It is unnatural, and yes counter intellectual, unscientific, even illiberal.

We sure have not seen signs of intellectual economic lives among the other political party, despite the full-time alien probing. In presence of intellectual candidates, they immediately retrograde to their designated underground cavities in search of new uninformed crews.

In a functioning democracy, the demonstrated infelicitousness of empathy will invite the luscious victory of the other party, unfortunately after some two years more languishing of real 10 to 25 percent unemployed and underemployed, and some 60 to 80 percent upset constituencies? We can even go back for the old fashion 6 month of nasty useless squabbling, called "election campaigns television seasons" to enrich the media Inc. Henceforth, for the betterment of America, and all good people, job-creation we must! Do not let them forget it. The 2014 and 2016 elections are almost here, even without jobs, you are getting the donation bills already.

Nevertheless, wealth-concentration and permanent wars economic schema are not free enterprise, free market strategies to create jobs or save USA middle class economy.

There are political monopolistic organizational arrangements like the morphed security industrial complex, which they have become self-leaking financial ice creams and they have not served the American economy well. They have longed abandoned serving the American people qualitatively, while they will claimed it quantitatively. For the successful economic model of wealth creation strategy, which Americans and the free market have done well many times in the history of modern economics.[1] Americans have to tend to the few main fundamental principles that served their constitutional democratic republic well, with relatively free markets principles.[2]

Nations have to invest and even reinvent domestic job-creations, exchange and value theory and balanced distributions systems, infrastructures, education systems, investors (immigrants' investors, scholars, job-creators), and cultivate domestic job creators.[3] In the democratic republic, the public can select new teams of representatives.

The New Year 2014 is foundational for a positive, reasonable, balanced futuristic, exceptional, and successful American economy model, which is a global economic model, since everyone is reading the same books.

Summary

The magnitude and clausal nature of demands for seven billion people on earth replaces much of callosity of obsolete paradigms of extreme dogma for the newer and softer sciences (economics and social and behavioral economics among them), which allow resource utilizations favoring human capital and renewable resources. Those combined with economic prudence in rate of entropy in utilization of finite and nonrenewable resources can light a newer longer path for such growing populations. In those endeavors and tasks, I do not see unemployment and idleness of different human capitals and skills levels, as much as presently bedevils our societies.

I wondered aloud here, if greed and politics of prejudices are at work, perhaps positive human capital interferences can improve and even remedy our futuristic conundrums. Americans cannot ignore President John F. Kennedy global efforts, and President Lyndon B. Johnson's 'American war on poverty'. Sargent Shriver, Eunice Kennedy Shriver, and Teddy Kennedy were the relentless and tireless advocacies that benefited USA greatly and globally. It is wonderful to see great efforts in continuum.[4] More renewed victories all earned, and deserved, will benefit Americans tenable structural, infrastructural accomplishments, with immigration and reemployment renewals above small-minded deteriorative and dysfunctional political squabbles.

The accumulations of my research and studies have shown me that such a progressive path can exists with strong probabilities. The readers have to see if that optimism can guide their paths to the future.

When time has aged you, and the youth have fled.

Not even a mystic can divine you, the mysteries of age.

When beauty has passed, and grace is in your head, and compassion has fled.

Not even a mystic can divine you, the mysteries of life.

Let stay human in your heart, and let the nesciences head flee.

Then even a mystic can divine you, the mysteries of love.

*Let knowledge find you, and let ignorance flee.
Then, a mystic will divine you the mysteries of your lives.*

Notes

[1] WHITE HOUSE Full Text of Obama's Speech on NSA Surveillance Delivered at the Justice Department on Friday, National Journal, January 17, 2014, http://www.nationaljournal.com/white-house/full-text-of-obama-s-speech-on-nsa-surveillance-20140117National Journal

[2] President Obama takes a step back from unfettered surveillance.
Doyle McManus, A new day at the NSA: President Obama takes a step back from unfettered surveillance, Los Angeles Times, Op-Ed, January 19, 2014,
http://www.latimes.com/opinion/commentary/la-oe-mcmanus-column-obama-surveillance-nsa-20140119,0,3116566,print.column latimes.com

[3] Dr. Bahman Fakhraie's books web page link, http://bahfecon.wix.com/bahfecon

[4] Sargent Shriver and peace corps efforts,
http://www.sargentshriver.org/gallery/the-peace-corps
http://www.cnn.com/2014/01/08/politics/war-on-poverty-50-years/index.html?utm_source=feedburner&utm_medium=feed&utm_campaign=Feed%3A+rss%2Fcnn_allpolitics+%28RSS%3A+Politics%29.
http://politicalticker.blogs.cnn.com/2014/01/13/obama-maria-shriver-to-talk-womens-poverty-issues/
http://shriverreport.org/

§§THE END§§

End Notes Summery

Dr. Bahman Fakhraie, © 2014, 2013,
Bahman Fakhraie, PhD UOU UT USA © 2011, 9-20-11
articles, Dr. Bahman Fakhraie's other articles
Notes,
TECONOMICS OF VERBALISM, EBook, Dr. Bahman Fakhraie
http://www.amazon.com/Teconomic-Of-Verbalism-ebook/dp/B00B1LO7UQ/ref=sr_1_4_title_0_main?s=books&ie=UTF8&qid=1360967834&sr=1-4&keywords=bahman+fakhraie
dspi: Disposable Personal Income (DSPI), Billions of Dollars, Monthly, Seasonally Adjusted Annual Rate
Job: usprvemp, USPRIV, All Employees: Total Private Industries (USPRIV), Thousands of Persons, Monthly, Seasonally Adjusted
Federal Reserve Economic Data
Link: http://research.stlouisfed.org/fred2
Help: http://research.stlouisfed.org/fred2/help-faq
Economic Research Division
Federal Reserve Bank of St. Louis
http://www.sltrib.com/sltrib/news/57223944-78/textbooks-university-utah-books.html.csp
More Notes
1-Teconomic of Verbalism,
https://www.createspace.com/4121720 *-
http://bahfecon.wix.com/bahfecon 1-
http://www.spiegel.de/international/world/obituary-nelson-mandela-dies-at-the-age-of-95-a-937581.html
2-
http://www.theguardian.com/world/2013/dec/06/mandela-funeral-worlds-most-powerful-us-iran-israeli-palestinian
3- http://www.washingtonpost.com/world/grief-deep-admiration-expressed-worldwide-for-the-revered-nelson-

mandela/2013/12/06/0d59755c-5e34-11e3-be07-006c776266ed_story.html?hpid=z2
4- http://www.nytimes.com/2013/12/06/world/africa/nelson-mandela_obit.html?ref=todayspaper&_r=0

Dr. Bahman Fakhraie's books:
1- Dr. Bahman Fakhraie, Teconomic Analysis of Cascading Millennial Economies
ISBN-97809852968,
https://www.createspace.com/4187823
2- Bahman Fakhraie, PhD., TECONOMICS OF VERBALISM
ISBN-978-0-9852958-4-4,
https://www.createspace.com/4121720
3- Bahman Fakhraie, PhD., DEMAND AND SUPPLY SIDES OF TECHNOLOGICAL INJECTIONS,
ISBN-978-0-9852958-3-7,
http://www.amazon.com/Demand-supply-Sides-Technological-Injections/dp/098529583X/ref=sr_1_4?ie=UTF8&qid=1360206619&sr=8-4&keywords=BAHMAN+FAKHRAIE
4- Bahman Fakhraie, PhD., TECONOMICS, Utah FERDAT Publishing 2012,
ISBN/EAN13: 0985295813 / 9780985295813,
https://www.createspace.com/4196760
5- Dr. Bahman Fakhraie, Teconomics of Dynamic Risks All Natural Disasters, And Energy Resource...,
ISBN/EAN13: 0985295856 / 9780985295851,
https://www.createspace.com/4282704
6-Dr. Bahman Fakhraie, Technological injection, dynamic new capital measurements, and Production Theory in Economics, (Michigan: ProQuest LLC, 2010) and, 94,
https://order.proquest.com/OA_HTML/pqdtibeCCtpItmDspRte.jsp

7- Dr. Bahman Fakhraie, TECONOMICS OF DYNAMIC SUSTAINABLE BUDGETS, Utah, Ferdat Publishing, 2013, http://www.amazon.com/...
8- Dr. Bahman Fakhraie, Teconomics of Dynamic Risks, Utah, Ferdat Publishing, 2013, http://www.amazon.com/Teconomics-oF-Dynamic-Risks
9- Dr. Bahman Fakhraie, POLITICAL MONOPOLISTIC CAPITALISM,
WEALTH CONCENTRATION SCHEMA, UNITED STATES TECONOMIC ANALYSIS, 2014, Utah, Ferdat Publishing, 2013, http://www.amazon.com/...
EBooks,
10- Dr. Bahman Fakhraie, TECONOMIC OF VERBALISM,
http://www.amazon.com/Teconomic-Of-Verbalism-ebook/dp/B00B1LO7UQ/ref=sr_1_4_title_0_main?s=books&ie=UTF8&qid=1360967834&sr=1-4&keywords=bahman+fakhraie#reader_B00B1LO7UQ6-
11- Dr. Bahman Fakhraie, Teconomics of Dynamic Risks, http://www.amazon.com/Teconomics-oF-Dynamic-Risks-ebook/dp/B00CUNPJZ6/ref=sr_1_1?s=digital-text&ie=UTF8&qid=1368893440&sr=1-1&keywords=Dr+bahman+fakhraie
Coming soon,
12- Bahman Fakhraie, PhD, TECONOMICS OF DYNAMIC SUSTAINABLE BUDGETS, Teconomic of Dynamic Sustainable Strategic Budgeting in X,
From Small to Large Operational Modular-Production growth Models.
https://www.createspace.com/4536462?ref=1147694&utm_id=6026
13- Bahman Fakhraie, POLITICAL MONOPOLISTIC CAPITALISM,
WEALTH CONCENTRATION SCHEMA, UNITED STATES TECONOMIC ANALYSIS, 2014, Utah, Ferdat Publishing, 2013,

http://www.amazon.com/s/ref=nb_sb_noss/182-0097772-9669123?url=search-alias%3Dstripbooks&field-keywords=dr%20bahman%20fkhraie%20print%20books#/ref=nb_sb_noss?url=search-alias%3Dstripbooks&field-keywords=Dr.+Bahman+Fakhraie&rh=n%3A283155%2Ck%3ADr.+Bahman+Fakhraie

Dr. Bahman Fakhraie's books web page link, http://bahfecon.wix.com/bahfecon

Appendix

In Memorial to two economic greats,

The advanced student of economic doctrine should know, I shared my thoughts with great Mrs. Robinson (Joan Robins, 1903-1983, Theory of Imperfect Competition, 1033). She was more than gracious and kind. She was very generous with her time and memories of post Keynes and Cambridge, United Kingdom, during her visit to University of Utah, Salt lake city, Utah, USA, in last millennium. She thought that the theoretical differences with Edward Chamberlin, 1966-1899 (Monopolistic Competition, 1933) were overworked. I like to acknowledge both of their contributions to economic science in memorial, (and social and behavioral sciences) and my thanks, and see here, she received more pen time.
Joan Robinson, Economist
Joan Violet Robinson FBA was a post-Keynesian economist who was well known for her work on monetary economics and wide-ranging contributions to economic theory. *Wikipedia*
Born, October 31, 1903, Surrey, United Kingdom
Died: August 5, 1983, Cambridge, United Kingdom
Education: Girton College, Cambridge, University of Cambridge
Dr. Edward Chamberlin, Economist
Edward Hastings Chamberlin was an American economist. He was born in La Conner, Washington, and died in Cambridge, Massachusetts. *Wikipedia*
Born, May 18, 1899, La Conner, WA. Died: July 16, 1967
Books: Towards a More General Theory of Value
Education: University of Michigan, Harvard University, University of Iowa

A
ARITHMATIC OF OPTIMIZATION

The series of mathematical analysis are presented henceforth, to study utility optimization and demand side, and production optimization and the supply side analysis. The traditional mathematical evaluation for optimization analysis is as follows:

Traditional productions function,

$$o = f(v_i^\varepsilon)$$

Necessary condition, it is also known as the first order condition (FOC):

$$f'(v_i^\varepsilon) > 0$$

Sufficient condition, it is also known as secondary condition (SOC):

$$f''(v_i^\varepsilon) > 0$$

The traditional production function is with mathematical evaluation for optimization analysis.

Conditions in Case of Growth

$$o = f(v_i^\varepsilon)$$
Necessary condition:
$$f'(v_i^\varepsilon) > 0$$
Sufficient condition:
$$f''(v_i^\varepsilon) > 0$$

Implication: the function is positive and increasing at the increasing rate.

Condition in Case of Decay

$$o = f(v_i^\varepsilon)$$
Necessary condition:
$$f'(v_i^\varepsilon) > 0$$
Sufficient condition:
$$f''(v_i^\varepsilon) < 0$$

Implication: the function is positive and increasing at the decreasing rate.

B

ARITHMATIC OF ENTREPRENEURIAL TIME

Lagrange analysis of n-variables and multi-constraints Lagrange multipliers the following is the mathematical analysis of productive use of available entrepreneurial times, on daily bases. Individuals have to make decision in time-use management, between productive choices they have to make in use of the fixed 24 hours given.

They make assumptive choices about their time uses, for required sleep, and time lot spent on education, and required work for income, as the following relations show. However, in post emergency, disaster, jobless times, other arrangements have to be made to replace the collateral plus time losses, and the income earned of time. Churches Mosques, Temples, and governmental and none governmental (NGOs) entities have had a historical rule.

$$f(X_S X_E X_W) = Q_i$$

$$g(X_S X_E X_W) = 24$$

$$h(X_S X_E X_W) = y_0$$

$$Z = f(X_S X_E X_W) + \mu[(24 - g(X_S X_E X_W))] + \gamma[(y_0 - h(X_S X_E X_W))] = 0$$

Qi = f(Xi)

g(Xi) = 24

h(Xi) = y_0

$Z\mu$ = 24 - g(Xi) = 0

$Z\gamma$ = y_0 - h(Xi) = 0

Zi = fi − μ gi - γ hi = 0

Arithmetical Proof:

FOC

$$\vartheta Z^1 = 0$$

SOC

$$\vartheta Z^2 < 0$$

All constants are great than zero.

C

MAXIMIZATION OF GAINS, OPTIMIZATION OF VALUE

Budget determines expenditure on costs of production of X, and Y. Y can be designated governmental, or NGO injection in new innovational capital, while X, is some local productions still operational, which must be encouraged to keep the level of economic activities high to accommodate the post technological-injection economy. $\lambda 1$ is unit costs.

$$B = \lambda 1\ X1 + \lambda 2 Y2$$

S denotes level of skills, technological injections required. In this example, $\lambda 2$ denotes the skill level of NGOs, or governmental units presented at the scene of disasters. In some nations, local skill or technologies are not able to present the type of presence, which the post disaster conditions demand. Geographically isolated areas require naval assets, which are not present in most countries to meet the logistic demands of post disaster conditions.

$$S = s1\ X2 + s2\ Y2$$

Education and retraining required in use capital productively.

$$E_k = e1\ k_X + e2\ k_Y$$

Production function is,

$$Q = f(X, Y : \dot{B}, \dot{S}, \dot{E})$$

The Lagrange equation is,

$$Z_Q = f(Vi) + \mu i\ [(\dot{B} - \lambda i\ Vi)] + \mu j\ [(\dot{S} - \lambda j\ Vj)] + \mu l\ [(\dot{E}_k - \lambda l\ Vl)]$$

FOC

$$dZ_Q/dt = 0$$

SOC

$$d^2 Z_Q / d^2 t < 0$$

More assumptive conditions are as follows,

All constants > 0

OPTIMIZATION OF VALUE

Optimization of Value Ψ is a function of maximization of profit, minimization of costs, and optimization of social welfare function of Vi.

$$\Psi = f(\max \Pi, \min C, \operatorname{opt} U_i)$$

$$U_i = f(q_{xi}, q_{yi} : C_{vi} : B_i, -/+?)$$

And

$$U_i = f(+, 0, -/+?)$$

COMPENSATORY SUSTAINABILITY CONDITIONS

Individual Utility Function

$$U_i = f(+, 0, -/+?)$$

The utility of individual Vi is improved in consumption of Qxi, while the consumption of Qyi stays the same, and the budget line can improve, stay the same, or become negative, thus also influencing the utility function.

Social Welfare Function of Group Utilities

$$\operatorname{Opt} SWF_{vi}, \quad SWF_{vi} = f(U_i, U_j, U_l, -/+?)$$

Majority of group utility will be better off at a new position A, therefore, they will agree to the project. The utility of some of group utility will stay the same. They stay either satisfy or join the last groups at position B. The utility of some of group will be worst off, there has to be tradeoffs, as in exchanges, higher remunerations, or tax-transfer strategies to optimize the experiences of all involved for them to agree to move to the better position A. This is another clause added to the arguments for sustainability conditions in all economic system orthodox or unorthodox, holistically.

SUSTIANABILITY CONDITIONS OF TECHNOLOGICAL INJECTIONS

Let us take a little time to study some of the sustainability conditions of investment in innovational new capital, with respect to social welfare functions for the group utility functions, for all individual in the group.

Two positions are A, and B, such that A is better than B.

$$A > B$$

Therefore, A is preferred to B,

$$\therefore A \, P \, B$$

$$SWFvi = f(Ui, Uj, Ul, -/+?)$$

The benefits sustainability conditions are as follows,

1. Sustainably condition universal criteria, it is if at least one individual utility function improves at A, others feel no change, then → A, A > B.

2. Sustainably condition Kaldorian criteria, this is when those in position A, pay, bribe, exchange with losers for the move to A, since A P B, then A > B. Alternatively, they offer to aid at their time of need.

3. Sustainably condition Hicks criteria, those losing from move to A, cannot bribe the groups to keep them from moving to A, therefore APB, → A, A > B.

4. Sustainably condition Scitovsky criteria, if the gainers can compensate (promise to help later) some of the losers. Moreover, some of the losers cannot bribe any of the winners from the move to A. The move will take place. Such that A P B, hence, →A, A>B.

5. Sustainably condition Dr. Bahman Fakhraie criteria, or the dynamic sustainably universal criteria, (NGOs or Gs assist production to operational levels) that technological injection will improve all utilities positions proportionally, such that [∀ U_i at A] P B, then →A, A>B. For some future post-functionality arrangements, (as tax and transfers).

There are more studies under welfare economic theory, and potential economic dissertational works.

D

RATES OF GROWTH AND DECAY

$$r^* = (Xt2-Xt1)/Xt1$$

$$r = \frac{\ln Xt2 - \ln Xt1}{\ln Xt1}$$

$$Ey, ms = \frac{\frac{\delta y}{\delta t}}{\frac{\delta ms}{\delta t}}$$

FERDAT, AND LEGALS
FAKHRAIE EDUCATION RESEARCH
DEVELOPMENT AND TRUST

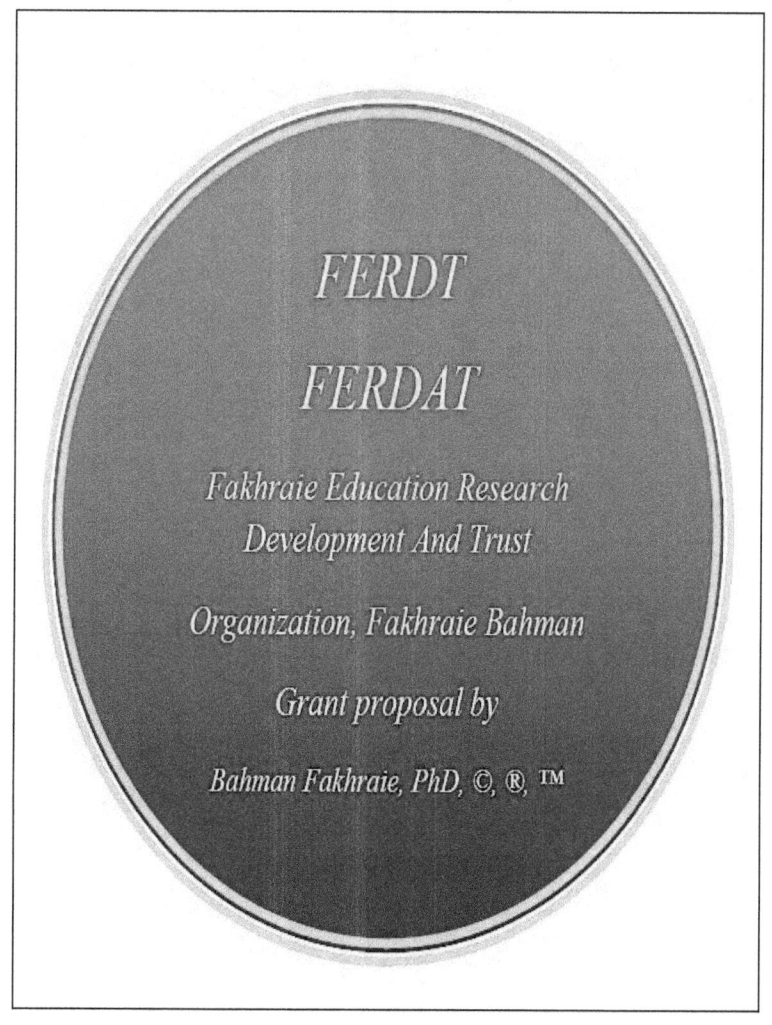

Budgetary, Managerial Directive and Legal Clauses

Legal letter and charges for unauthorized information use.

Section 1, Mission Statement

Section 2, Budgetary Clause

Section 3, Managerial Clause

Section 4, Legal Clause

Section 5, Organization Chart

Section 6, Data Management

Section 7, Vita

Legal letter is in cases of e-fraud, misuse of firms' information, or harm under sec. G. All linked and relaying entities, institutions, governmental agencies are accountable no exception.

Dear Sirs, persons, INC., (illegal use of firms' info), your current bill is **$10,000, ≤Ceiling $60 mils.** On behalf of Dr. Bahman Fakhraie, FERDAT, and the firm, family trusts.

These are the current charges related to illegal e-fraud and all harmful misuse of firms information, after the first time we asked you to terminate all contract and remove our name, firms' name etc. on this date.

1-Illegal use, the unapproved initial use of firm's name, contact name, duns #, any and all information supplied to USA government for the sole purpose of firm doing business with USA government, grant.gov, and NSF, Universities, other governmental and tribal entities, and all grantors. Minimum charges are $10,000.00, up to the ceiling of $ 60 million.

2-Use of firm contacts, names, address phone #, TIN/#s, and any information related to that.

Minimum charges are $10,000.00, up to the ceiling of $60 mils.

3- Continuation after repeated formal request to terminate illegal actions, sending junk e-mail, junk mail, forcing this firm to send back, by mail and certified mail. Legal costs related to that.

Minimum charges are $10,000.00 per each event, up to the ceiling of $60 mils.

4- Interference with firm soul business, time sensitive writing of government and private grants, at grant.gov, and NSF, universities, private foundations, NGOs and all grantors, with 4.5 million dollars floor. The Minimum charges are 4.5 million dollars, up to the ceiling of $60 mils.

4- Absolute or required non-disclosures by the firm or Dr. Fakhraie will require pre-paid plan with minimum flooring pay. Flex-legalism targeted at the firm, or Dr. B. Fakhraie will be due cause for nonpaid termination by the same, and harm-terms of Sec G of private contracts.

6- Punitive damages are up to 60 million dollars, if you do not stop, after the first notification.

Please make an effort to pay your bill. There will be additional charges added and sent to you for each time you try to contact the same entities, after the same dated termination notices.

Dr. BF, this is part of the legal notices under sec G, or formal termination notice dates.

Section 1, Mission Statement
To formulate optimum functionality in management teams, in order to make profitable and beneficial contributions, and create opportunity for merited advancements, **to advance research** in my fields of study. Utilizing rare combination of theory and empiricism, cultivated in multi-cultural inclusive settings in academic and private enterprises, I enhance the management in productivity and completion of productive projects, or suggest corrective recursive evaluation and total quality control improvements.

Experiences, among fields of International Trade, Managerial, and Production theories in Economics, Finance, Personal Finance management, and Businesses, which modern business and academic institutions find very expensive to employ and too costly not to employ. My extensive backgrounds help me advance research in my fields of study.

Section 2, Budgetary Clause
* All initial dedicated deposits (inflows) will be transferred to a FREDT, or FREDAT business account.

* No allotments or contracts activity will take place, until full transfer of funds has taken place per contracts. The cash-accounting method is used for tax purposes.
* **Alteration to submit to requirements and regulations will fully transfer all risks, fees, and penalties, and legal responsibilities, to the source of the requirements.**
* There will be a minimum product list, or writing, or proposal-output for further research, which will be presented and agreed to at the initial phases.
* This will be the only output legally required at the end of contract, or at the end of grant periods.
* There is a managerial flow chart enclosed to enhance comprehensions of cash flow, read after the legal notes section.

Section 3, Managerial Clause
* Dr. Bahman Fakhraie will act as agent, manger, and soul administrator, Executives director, Principle Investigator PI for FERDT, FERDAT, Fakhraie Bahman Organization, with full rights to take legal action and make final settlement on its accounts.
* Dr. Bahman Fakhraie will act as agent, manger, and soul administrator for Fakhraie Bahman Organization, with full right to take legal action on its accounts.
* A general electronic bookkeeping is followed, on periodical bases, as grants require it. Current standard is quarterly, post full disbursements of grant funding. (FRR is required quarterly)
* Details, information, managerial technologies are legally protected, and no such disclosure will be made of the Organization, administrator, assignees, or representatives of FERDT, FERDAT, or Fakhraie Bahman Organization. All copyright materials are

marketable, or further developed by Mr. Fakhraie. All existing rights are reserved.
* All informal and formal requests can be made by mail, or email.
* There is forfeiture of all advances, in cases of mortality, health, or attempt at disbarment, legal action, harm, against soul administrator, Fakhraie Bahman Organization, with full right to take legal action on its accounts.
* Any and all such request will have to forward additional funding for legal representations and undue imposition of costs or harm, please read the legal note and sec. G. It will always apply.
* **Alteration to submit to requirements and regulations will fully transfer all risks, fees, and penalties, and legal responsibilities, to the source of the requirements.**
* The reviewers will have access to a portion of the progress.
* Full transparencies are practiced for authorized agents only, mostly through the internet, after proper signatures are obtained.
* All future development, educational development will have to be contracted, or signed out temporarily.
* All copyrights and proprietary rights are reserved, granted, accorded to Dr. Bahman Fakhraie, and his living trust.
* The final product in initial agreement will be shared with the grantors, after all the financial settlements have been met.

- PI, FERDAT; Dr. Fakhraie, Bahman
  Dr. Bahman Fakhraie, PhD, UOU, UT, USA
- Position Classification, Executive level I,
- Salary exceeds Fed Cap for private contracts.
- NSF ID, 000586796, Organizational ID Code, P 269878425
- Private for Profit Business:
- DUNS Number D&B # ▅▅▅89684,
- CAGE/NCAGE: ▅▅S3, Congressional Districts, UT_001
- Sec G of private contract always applies
- For other institutional DUNS, etc. Please, check cover letter, or contact PI. Thanks
- PI Information(dated)

Grantors information goes here

Section 4, Legal Clause, All Right Reserved & Other Legal Notes
All rights will revert to author after 3 years, if limited rights are contracted.
E. Speech, Lecture Tours, and Research Papers & Follow Up:
All publications or Grant-products are commonly published on completion, USA Library of Congress, Trade Journals, Or Author's websites, etc.
Contact for individualized contracts
F. for Time Donation, And Charity Events: 1. 5% of Net contracts paid 2. Time by Appointments Only. 3. Write Donations Checks to Fakhraie Trust fund / Bahman Fakhraie
G. Any and All Risks or Harms invokes these legal clauses. The Following legal clauses are base minimum, and will not limit all rights and legal protection, with uniform constitutional rights they are implied and accorded. Contractually all rights are implied and accorded. Please, read all the legal notes before using any materials.

G1. In Cases of misuse of these materials, plagiarisms, use to put at risk of harm, or to harm, (Legal, or Etc.) the firm, CEO, FERDT, president: Mr. Bahman Fakhraie, His family members, it will result in $60 million legal action per each event in United States Courts/ any Jurisdictions determined or set by author or a trust set up by Mr. Bahman Fakhraie. Also, use of creative ideas and intellectual properties for any commerce direct or indirect or by proxy, expansions of outlines, attempts to defraud, over charge, harm with illegal acts, misuse of private and confidential materials, information, and properties, letters, checks, e-mails, faxes, any and all communications, and any electronically stored materials and pictures, or false claims against the above entities will be an agreement with and subject to all elements of this contract, and as a user license, without nullifying further and ensuing legal actions or collections, or as directed by the same or authorities. All other contracts are one time contracts and s. t. this contract. Please, notify firm, Mr. Bahman Fakhraie, of all infractions, transactions, or transfer to individuals or to private or government entities in accord with current laws.

G2a. All Costs due to inquiries, related or required business licenses, legal paper works, and hours, all costs related to corrective or reparation publicity, bonding and insurances costs, stock related activities, all costs related to any harm (financial & legal) will be charges to the sources and inquirers, and none to the firm or Bahman Fakhraie, his family, or any and all of their related assets. All attempts to harm, engagements, cashing checks or accepting cash from the same entities is an agreement with all elements of this contract.

G2b. All copy rights associated with written works and further development of all works remains with the author Bahman Fakhraie or his trusts. All development rights are reserved by the same entities.

G3. Any and all unsolicited commercial phone calls, to Mr. Bahman Fakhraie and, his family will result to a minimum of $ 500 per call charged to the source, due and payable in the same month the call is made, all other elements of this contract also apply, all contracts remain subservient to this contract, all costs of collection and legal actions also are added to the bill payable by source and not Bahman Fakhraie and these entities.

G4.All Consultation and coaching involves risks due to market, business, political, etc. costs and damages related to all such risk are paid by individuals or business entities involved and none is implied or taken by Bahman Fakhraie, his family, or any related assets, under any and all conditions. These entities' court fees are $10,000; et minimum.

G5. Uncomfortable conditions, misapplications of any law to harm, harassment, odd-hour calls, etc will be due cause for termination of services without refund, and are actionable per this contract.

§§§§

All Right Reserved & Other Legal Notes

All publications or Grant-products are published on completion, USA Library of Congress, Trade Journals, Or Author's websites, etc. All rights revert to author after 3 years, if limited rights are contracted.

E. Speech, Lecture Tours, Research Papers & Follow Up:
1. Per Each Event-$ 350,000 +.
2. with Foreign Travel-$ 3,000,000
3. Book/Cash Advance floor Min; Net Royalties ~40%
4. Scripts: /Starting from.....................$ 300,000
5. Movie Script (120+Pages).................$ 3,000,000
6. Or Cash Advance Plus 2% of All Gross paid annually
7. Consultations Fee/Initial charge non-refunded $ 10,000, & ...10 %
8. Business limited ventures, partnerships, etc. .... ≥ 30%
9. Salary executive level I

F. for Time Donation, And Charity Events: 1. 5% of Net contracts paid 2. Time by Appointments Only.3. Write Donations Checks to Fakhraie Trust fund / Bahman Fakhraie. G. Any and All Risks or Harms invokes these legal clauses. The Following legal clauses are base minimum, and will not limit all rights and legal protection, with uniform constitutional rights they are implied and accorded. Contractually all rights are implied and accorded. Please, read all the legal notes before using any materials. G1. In Cases of misuse of these materials, plagiarisms, use to put at risk of harm, or to harm, (Legal, or Etc.) the firm, CEO: Mr. Bahman Fakhraie, His family members, will result in $60 million legal action per each event in United States Courts/Jurisdictions determine by author or a trust set up by Mr. Bahman Fakhraie. Also, use of creative ideas intellectual properties, expansions of outlines, attempts to defraud, over charge, harm with illegal acts, misuse of private and confidential materials and properties, letters, e-mails, faxes, any and all communications, and any electronically stored materials and pictures, or false claims against the above entities will be an agreement with all elements of this contract, and as a use license, without nullifying ensuing legal actions or collections, or as directed by the same or authorities. Please, notify firm, Mr. Bahman Fakhraie, of all infractions, transactions, or transfer to individuals or to private or government entities. G2a. All Costs due to inquiries, related or required business licenses, legal paper works and hours, all costs related to corrective or reparation publicity, bonding and insurances costs, stock related activities, all costs related to any harm (financial & legal) will be charges to the sources and inquirers, and none to the firm or Bahman Fakhraie, his family, or any and all of their related assets. All attempts to harm, engagements, cashing checks or accepting cash from the same entities is an agreement with all elements of this contract. G2b. All copy rights associated with written works and further development of all works remains with the author Bahman Fakhraie or his trusts. Any and all development rights are reserved by the same entities. G3. Any and all unsolicited commercial phone calls to Mr. Bahman Fakhraie, his family will result to a minimum of $ 500 per call charged to the source, due and payable in the same month the call is made, all other elements of this contract also apply, all contracts remain subservient to this contract, all costs of collection and legal actions also are added to the bill payable by source and not Bahman Fakhraie and these entities. G4.All Consultation and coaching involves risks due to market, business, political, etc. costs and damages related to all such risk are paid by individuals or business entities involved and none is implied or taken by Bahman Fakhraie, his family, or any related assets, under any and all conditions. These entities' court fees are $10,000; et minimum. G5.Uncomfortable conditions, misapplications of any law to harm, harassment, odd-hour calls, etc. will be due cause for termination of services without refund, and are actionable per this contract.

§§§§

Letter of Agreement with FRDET and Fakhraie Bahman

I/We (Ms., Mrs., Mr.): ....

Business Name: ....

Social Security numbers: ....../......./............   ..../......./................

Tax ID Numbers: ....

Driver License Numbers:
....

Passport (Birth Certificate) Numbers:
....

Have read all the information supplied by Dr. Bahman Fakhraie, and /or FRDET (Trust, LLP). Agree to supply all correct financial and related information and select the following services by marking (X), or Letter a b c, Or Number 1 2 3, or write and specify. Agree to the power of attorney required to confirm or acquire financial and related information. Plus a check for $3000, for preliminary registrations, legal and financial inquiries, and licensing fees.

1: ☐   2: ☐   3: ☐   4: ☐   5: ☐   6: ☐   7: ☐   8: ☐

Specify which kinds of the following accounts you will require:
Individual/Gov. ☐   Joints ☐   Joint with survival rights ☐   Trusts ☐
  Details: ....

Business types:
  Ltd Partnership (LLP, LLC) ☐   Soul Owner ☐
  Inc/Gov ☐   Firm ☐
    Details: ....

I/We agree to pay the fees and costs as they accrue, after 30 days a charge of %10 per annum is added to past due amounts until they are settled or paid in full. That at least 75% charges and expenses are paid no later than six month after initial reports or outlines are examined. That all travel lodgings and phone charges, legal research, and research hours, I/We request are fully paid. I/We have read and understand the nature of business, business cycles, market price fluctuation risks, currency fluctuation risks, social and political risks, natural and climatic risks, and all other risks herewith not itemized; therefore, I/we accept all financial losses, responsibilities, all punitive or compensatory damages that occur for all activities that are undertaken based on or claimed related to the report or reports, advise and etc., generated by Money Wise Firm, Bahman Fakhraie or all the entities named, agents, and associates. I/We understand in cases of any false, misleading, or withholding information the Money Wise Firm and all entities named above will not be held accountable, responsible, financially or otherwise, and will be refunded for any damages fully. I/We release all others associated with Money Wise Firm, and Bahman Fakhraie from financial losses, responsibilities, all compensatory and punitive charges concerning activities I/We undertake.

Sign (full name, titles, and address)
 Business (Name, Address; Agents' title):

Section 5, Organization Chart

⇔Requests for grants, grant and contract proposals and Minimums contracted output Grant Funds, ⇓ Organization DUNS, University DUNS ⇓ Administrator ⇒FRDAT
⇓
FERDAT & FERDAT- C
Publishing and Production
President, Administrator, Executive level 1
⇓
Bahman Fakhraie, PhD, © 2011, UOU, UT, USA
®, ™
Tasks and controls, TQC, and Redo, Recycles
⇔Tax and expense disbursements
⇓
Completed project Vs. Minimums contracted output
⇔ Informal notification of source of funds, with future project proposal if any,
⇒Formal and final notification from FRDET, FERDAT
⇔ Final confirmation of conclusion from Administrators
⇒ Final confirmation of conclusion from Organization Fakhraie
⇔ Keeping communication and network open to future project.
Bahman Fakhraie, PhD, © ® ™ 2010-, UOU, UT, USA

Section 6, DATA MANAGEMENT:

Relevant data will be managed, and stored. Moreover, the data and the progression of data used will be stored post completion. As a common practice, Dr. Bahman Fakhraie will, also preserve a historical over view of data for legal purposes, for future use. A portion of that will be shared if requested in written form, post settlement of all expenses. The ethical requirements will be followed in accordance with the applied law established.

The final product will be shared with the grantors, after all the financial settlements have been met. The reviewers will have access to a portion of the progress. All publications or Grant-products are published on completion for academic and educational research, USA Library of Congress, trade journals, FERDAT Publishing, author's websites, other academic journals, etc.

All rights will revert to author after 3 years, if contract exits for limited rights.

Labor laws and benefit distribution will be according to the institutional Fed Cap limits, private contracts; vendors are responsible for their own legal obligations. (Publication Ink, FedExx, kinkcos, vendors etc.)

CPA and Legal establishment, outside to this entity will be contracted to handle more complex issues when they arise, all cost are due, prior to any such required actions are requested.

Full transparencies are practiced for authorized agents only, mostly through the internet, after proper signatures are obtained. All copyrights and proprietary rights are granted, accorded and reserved to Dr. Bahman Fakhraie,

All future development, educational development will have to be contracted, or signed out temporarily, they will revert to Dr. Bahman Fakhraie, in case of all legal issues.

These and other clauses will be amended and upgraded as required over time, they all apply.

Absolut or required non-disclosures by the firm or Dr. Fakhraie will require pre-paid plan with minimum flooring pay. Flex-legalism targeted at the firm, or Dr. B. Fakhraie will be due cause for nonpaid termination by the same.

G. Any and All Risks or Harms invokes these legal clauses. The Following legal clauses are base minimum, and will not limit all rights and legal protection, with uniform constitutional rights they are implied and accorded. Contractually all rights are implied and accorded. Please, read all the legal notes before using any materials.

Sec 7, Check CURRICULUM VITA

SELECTED BIBLIOGRAPHY

Bailey, Martin J. *National Income and the Price Level: A Study in Macroeconomic Theory,* New York, McGraw-Hill, 1971.

Baumol, William J. *Economic Theory and Operational Analysis,* 4th ed., New Jersey: Prentice-Hall, 1977.

Blaug, Mark, *Economic Theory in Retrospect,* 3rd Ed., London: The Cambridge University Press, 1978.

Böhn_Bawerk, Eugen Von. *Capital and Interest: Positive Theory of Capital,* vol. II, Trans. G. D. Hunt & H. F. Sennholz, Chicago: Libertarian Press, 1959.

Boulding, Kenneth E. *Economics As A science*, New York: McGraw-Hill Book Company, 1970.

Byers, Lloyd L. *Concept of Strategic Management: Planning and Implementation*, New York: Harper & Row Publishers

Caves, Richard E. and Jones, R. W. *World Trade and Payments: An Introduction,* 2nd ed. Boston, Little, Brown and Company, 1977

Chiang, Alpha C. *Fundamental Methods of Mathematical Economics*, 2nd ed., New York: McGraw-Hill Book Company, 1974.

Coombs, Philip H. *The World Educational Crisis: A System Analysis*, London: Oxford University Press, 1968.

Domar, Evsey D. *Essays in the Theory of Economic Growth*, New York: Oxford University Press, 1957, 154-167, 168, 181.

Druker, Peter F. *Innovation and Entrepreneurship*, New York: Harper & Row Publishers, 1985.

Eisner, R. "Depreciation Allowances, Replacement Requirement, and Growth," *The American Economic Review*, XLII, December 1952.

Dr. Bahman Fakhraie, *Teconomics of Dynamic Risks All Natural Disasters, And Energy Resource...*
ISBN/EAN13:   0985295856 / 978098529585
https://www.createspace.com/4282704

EBook link: http://www.amazon.com/Teconomics-oF-Dynamic-Risks-ebook/dp/B00CUNPJZ6/ref=sr_1_1?s=digital-text&ie=UTF8&qid=1368893440&sr=1-1&keywords=Dr+bahman+fakhraie

Bahman Fakhraie, PhD., *TECONOMICS,*
ISBN/EAN13:   0985295813 / 9780985295813,
https://www.createspace.com/4196760

—. *TECONOMIC OF VERBALISM,* Utah, FERDAT publishing 2012, and
Paperback link is at, https://www.createspace.com/4121720
The EBook Link is at,
http://www.amazon.com/dp/B00B1LO7UQ
Books web page at, http://bahfecon.wix.com/bahfecon#

—. The Demand and Supply Sides of Appropriate Technological Advancement, (Research paper at University of Utah Economics Dept. 2003)

—. *Demand and supply Sides of Technological Injections*, Utah, FERDAT Publishing, 2004, And at, http://www.amazon.com/dp/098529583X/ref=rdr_ext_tmb #reader_098529583X

—. *Technological injection, dynamic new capital measurements, and Production Theory in Economics*, (Michigan: ProQuest LLC, 2010) and, https://order.proquest.com/OA_HTML/pqdtibeCCtpItmDspRte.jsp

—. Books, paperbacks & EBooks web page, http://bahfecon.wix.com/bahfecon#

—. *Teconomics of Verbalism*, Utah FERDAT Publishing 2012, and at, https://www.createspace.com/4121720, Books web page at, http://bahfecon.wix.com/bahfecon#

—. *Analytical Remedies for The Millennial Cascading Economic Declines*, Utah FERDAT Publishing 2012, and at, https://www.createspace.com/4187823,
Books web page at, http://bahfecon.wix.com/bahfecon

—. "Economic Theories and Practices in Technological Changes, capital measures, and Production." (Research paper at University of Utah Economics Dept. 1988)

—. "Hallowing headless nations: the need to invest on public education under the 1980s international economic conditions," (Research paper at University of Utah Economics Dept. 1988)

—. "Transfer of Technologies and Socioeconomic Theories of Dualism," (Research paper at University of Utah Economics Dept. 1983)

Friedman, Milton and Schwartz, Anna Jacobson, *The Great Contraction 1929-1933*, vol.2, 2nd ed., New Jersey: Princeton University Press, 1973

Gander, James Patrick, *Technological Change and Raw Materials*, Salt Lake City: Bureau of Economic and Business Research, University of Utah, 1977.

Gardner, Ackley, *Macroeconomics: Theory and Policy*, New York: Macmillan Publishing Co., 1978.

Girton, Lance and Roper Don, "Theory and Implication of Currency Substitution," *Journal of Money, Credit, and Banking,* 13, no. 1 (February 1981): 12-30.

Hayek, Friedrich August Von. "Kapitalaufzehrung." Weltwirtschaftliches Archive 36, 1932, II, 86-108.

Heilbroner, Robert L. *The Worldly Philosophers*, New York: Time Inc., Special Ed., 1962.

Hicks, Sir John, *The Crisis in Keynesian Economics*, New York: Basic Books, Inc. 1974.

Hirshleifer, Jack, *Investment, Interest, and Capital*, New Jersey: Prentice-Hall, 1970.

—. *Time, Uncertainty, and Information*, New York: Basil Blackwell, 1989.

—. *Price Theory and Applications*, New Jersey: Prentice-Hall, 1976.

Henderson, J. M. and Quandt, R. E. *Microeconomic Theory; A Mathematical Approach*, 2nd ed., New York: McGraw-Hill, 1972. 191-199, 280

Hunt, E. K. and Howard J. Sherman, *Economics: An Introduction to Traditional and Radical Views*, 2nd Ed., San Francisco: Harper and Row Publishers, 1975.

Hutchinson, H. D. *Money, Banking, And The United States Economy*, 3rd. ed. New jersey, Englewood Cliffs, Prentice-Hall, Inc. 1975

Intriligator, Michael D. *Econometric Models, Techniques, and Applications*, New Jersey: Prentice-Hall, 1978.

Johnson, J. *Econometric Methods*. New York: McGraw-Hill, 1972.

Kant, Immanuel, *Critique of Judgment*, Trans. J. H. Bernard, New York: Hafner, 1951.

Kennedy Charles and Thirlwall, A.P. "Surveys in Applied Economics: Technological Progress," *The Economic Journal*, March 1972: 12.

Keynes, John Maynard, *Essays in Biography*, London: The Cambridge University Printing House for Royal Economic Society, 1972.

—. *The General Theory of Employment, Interest and Money,* 1st ed. 1936, London: The Cambridge University Printing House for Royal Economic Society, Reprint 1973.

Kindleberger, Charles P. *The World in Depression 1929-1939*, Los Angeles: University of California Press, 1973.

Kirzner, I.M. *Discovery and the Capitalist Process*, Chicago: University of Chicago Press, 1985.

Klein, P. A. and Moore, G. H., *Monitoring Growth Cycles in Market-Oriented Countries*, (Mass.: published for N. B. E. R., by Ballinger publishing Co., 1985).

Knight, Farnk H. *Risk, Uncertainty and Profit*, Chicago: University of Chicago Press, 1985.

Landes, David S. *The wealth and poverty of nations: Why Some are So Rich and Some are So Poor*, (New York: W.W. Norton & Company, 1998).

Lindert, Peter H. and Kindleberger Charles P., *International Economics,* 7th Ed., Illinois: Richard Irwin, 1982.

Mansfield, Edwin, *Technological Change*, New York: W. W. Norton & Co., 1971.

Mark, Blaug, *Economic Theory in Retrospect*, 3rd Ed. London: The Cambridge University Press, 1978.

Marx, K. (In a letter he wrote to Engel, dated 20 August, 1862, London), (handout by Professor Randa, 2004)

McKinnon, Ronald I. *Money and Capital in Economic Development*, Washington D. C.: The Brookings Institution, 1973.

Mensch, Gerhard, Das *technilogische Patt.*, Frankfurt: Umschau Verlag, 1975.

—, *Stalemate in Technology: innovation overcome the Depression*, (Massachusetts: Ballinger Publishing Company, 1979).

Miles, T.R. "Gestalt Theory," in The Encyclopedia of Philosophy, New York: Macmillan Publishing Co., vols. 3 and 4, 1967.

Mishan, Edward Joshua, *Cost-Benefit Analysis,* 4th Ed. London: Unwin Hyman, 1988.

Moran, Michael. "New England Transcendentalism," in The Encyclopedia of Philosophy, (New York: Macmillan Publishing Co., Vols. 3 and 4, 1967).

Mundell, Robert A. "Growth, Stability, and Inflationary Finance," Journal *of Political Economy*, 73, 1963.

Pindyck, R.S. and Rubinfeld, D.L., *Econometric Models and Econometric*, 2nd ed., New York: McGraw-Hills, 1981.

Ott, J. Steven, *The Organizational Culture Perspectives*, (Pacific Grove, California: Brooks/Cole Publishing Company, 1989).

Quirk, James and Saposnik, Rubin, *Introduction to General Equilibrium Theory and Welfare Economics*, New York: McGraw-Hill, 1968.

Rima, Ingrid, *Development of Economic Analysis*, 7th ed., New York: Routledge, 2009.

Rodinson, M. *Islam and Capitalism*, Trans. B. Pearce, Austin: University of Texas, 1981.

Rosenberg, Nathan, Technology *and American Economic Growth*, New York: M. E. Sharp, 1972.

Ruttan, V. W. "Usher and Schumpeter on Invention, and Technological Change," Quarterly *Journal of Economics*, 1960, 602

Ruttan, Vernon W. "Usher and Schumpeter on Invention, Innovation, and Technological change," Quarterly *Journal of Economics*, 1960, 73

Samuelson, Anthony Paul. *Economics*, 11th Ed., New York: McGraw-Hill, 1980.

Savich, R.S. and Thomson, L. A. *Resource Allocation within the Product Life Cycles*, Business Topic, MSU: MSU, fall 1978.

Schmooker, Jacob, *Invention and Economic Growth*, Massachusetts: Harvard University Press, 1966.

Schultz, Theodore W. *Investing in People: The Economics of Population Quality*, Berkley: University of California Press, 1982.

Schumpeter, Joseph A. *Business Cycles*, vol. 1. New York: McGraw Hill Book Company, 1939.

—. *Business Cycles: A Theoretical, Historical, and Statistical Analysis of the Capitalists Process,* vol. I, New York, McGraw Hill Book Company, 1938.

—. *The Theory of Economic Development: An Inquiry into Profits, Capital, Credit, Interest, and Business Cycle*, Trans., Redvers Opie, London: Oxford University Press, Reprint 1980.

Smith, Adam. *An Inquiry into the Nature and Cause of Wealth of Nations*, Edited by E. Cannon, Chicago: University of Chicago Press, 1976.

—. *An Inquiry into the Nature and Causes of Wealth of Nations*, vol. 2, 2nd ed., Oxford: the Clarendon Press, 1988.

—. *The Theory of Moral Sentiments*, London, 1st ed., 1757.

Smith, E.J. Chambers, R.H. Scott and R.S. *National Income Analysis and Forecasting*, Glenview: Scott, Foresman and Company, 1975.

Spiegle, Henry William. *The Growth of Economic thought*, North Carolina: Duke University Press, 1983.

Stigler, George J. *The Theory of Price*, 3rd ed., New York: The Macmillan Company, 1966.

Takaki, Ronald, *A Different Mirror: A History of Multicultural America*, London: Little Brown and Company, 1993.

Taylor, John R., *An Introduction to Error Analysis*, Mill Valley: University Science Books, 1982.

Thirtle, Colin G. and Ruttan V. W. *The Role of Demand and Supply in the Generation of Diffusion of Technological Change*, Switzerland, 1987.

U. S. President, *Economic Report of the President*, (Washington, D.C.: Government printing office, 1990)

Usher, Abbot Payson, *A History of Mechanical Inventions*, London: Oxford University Press, 1954.

Usher, Abbot Payson, *A History of Mechanical Inventions*, Revised ed., London: Oxford University Press, 1954.

Viner, Jacob, *Studies in the Theories of International Trade*, New York: Harper and Brothers publishers, 1937.

Wainwright, A. C. Chiang and K., *Fundamental Methods of Mathematical Economics*, 4th ed., Boston: McGraw-Hill Irwin, 2005.

Webster, Merriam, *Merriam-Webster's Collegiate Dictionary*, 9th ed., Springfield: M.W. Inc., 1985.

Young, Hugh D. *Statistical Treatment of Experimental Data*, New York: McGraw-Hill, 1962.

CURRICULUM VITA

Bahman Fakhraie, PhD, UOU, UT, USA
University Of Utah, Economic Dept., U. O. U.;   Salt Lake City, Utah USA, 84112
Permanent Address: c/o 1120 Canyon Rd No. 29; Ogden Utah 84404
E-Mail: bf9@utah.edu , bahf.econ@gmail.com, dr.bahf.econ@gmail.com
Dr. Bahman Fakhraie's Books webpage, http://bahfecon.wix.com/bahfecon

Honors and Awards: **Omicron Delta Epsilon Honor Society**
Utah State U. USA, **Certificates Keys to Agricultural Development at the Local Level**
Student Leadership Positions: **President of International Student Association** [ASUSU]

Bachelor of Science:	**Utah State University**
Master of Science:	**Utah State University**
PhD, University of Utah	**University of Utah**

PhD, Economics (international economics), University of Utah

Certificate of Completion, PhD in Economics University of Utah, 2010
Certificate of Completion, PhD in Economics University of Chicago, 2011

Mission Statement:
To formulate optimum functionality in management teams, in order to make profitable and beneficial contributions, and create opportunity for merited advancements. Utilizing rare combination of theory and empiricism, cultivated in multi-cultural inclusive settings in academic and private enterprise, I enhance the productivity and completion of project management. Experiences, among

fields of International Trade, Managerial, and Production theories in Economics, Finance, and Business, which modern business and academic institutions find very expensive to employ and too costly not to employ. The extensive background helps advance research in my field of study.

Goals:
I have initiated, passed, and funded many constructive projects --goals by committees--, where it has been value enhancing and mutually beneficial individually, and by team assists. Private Senior Economist: Research Positions with Contracts, Teaching, Research, Books, with contract.

Short Term Private Contracts are for economic and financial educational consultations.

Academic Preparatory Continuum:

PhD, University of Utah, Dissertation:
TECHNOLOGICAL INJECTION, DYNAMIC NEW CAPITAL MEASUREMENTS AND PRODUCTION THEORY IN ECONOMICS

Thesis statement:
The dynamic influences of technology and elemental factors of production --defined and measured in this dissertation-- are greater than commonly have been calculated or expected. The impacts of different measurements of capital stocks (traditional and new adjusted capital) on embodied and disembodied technological variables, on productivity, and economic growth of national social products are tested. The econometric effects of two new capital stock measures introduced in the writing of Friedrich August Von Hayek, John Maynard Keynes, and further developed by Evsey D. Domar, and ignored by most modern economists are examined. Therefore, we focus on the demand and supply side of technological embodied in capital, in human skill and produced goods and services, and the economy. Dr.

Bahman Fakhraie's Book-link is at,
https://order.proquest.com/OA_HTML/pqdtibeCCtpItmDspRte.jsp

Post-Doctoral Research and Goals:
1. Updating the econometrics of the dissertation to most recent available data and dates, (per available grants)
2. Include, countries, with acceptable data in the study, set up formulaic development in excel etc. for use. (per grants)
3. Focus on the theoretical advancement in production processes for systemic innovational additive methodologies, in Movie production, Agriculture, and other creative industries, using existing or newly hired faculties, in anchored and linked institutions. This is a great serious work in shadows of Adam Smith, Schumpeter, Hayak, and Keynes.

Teconomics: Scientific Synthesis of Economics and Technology in Teconomics

4. Stream line methodologies, and project for PhD Students, master students, and introductory fields' level, an extension of the dissertation and current copyrighted writings.
5. A multimedia production of Dr. Fakhraie's recent research,
NEW DYNAMIC ECONOMIC MODELS TO STUDY TECHNOLOGY INJECTIONS & DYNAMIC CAPITAL FORMATION, IMPACTS ON INTERNATIONAL TRADE, EXCHANGE RATE, AND GLOBAL ECONOMIC OPTIMASATION

Presentation by Dr. Bahman Fakhraie
6. Of course, this will be under Sec G of private contract and without infringing on rights of marketing, publishing, and distribution of the same.

Certain contracts will be more restrictive, including specific names.
7. Finish the books series in post dissertation Teconomic studies, Micro, Macro, Teconometrics, Teconomic Analysis, and Political Teconomics. (in progress)

Books, published: DR. Bahman Fakhraie's Books web page at, http://bahfecon.wix.com/bahfecon

Dr. Bahman Fakhraie, *TECONOMIC OF VERBALISM,* Utah, FERDAT publishing 2012, a
Paperback link is at, https://www.createspace.com/4121720
The EBook Link is at,
http://www.amazon.com/dp/B00B1LO7UQ
Books web page at, http://bahfecon.wix.com/bahfecon

- *Demand and supply Sides of Technological Injections*, Utah, FERDAT Publishing, 2004, And at,
http://www.amazon.com/dp/098529583X/ref=rdr_ext_tmb reader_098529583X

- *Teconomics: the microeconomic analysis*, Utah, FERDAT publishing 2012, and, https://www.createspace.com/4196760, Books web page at,
  http://bahfecon.wix.com/bahfecon

- *Technological injection, dynamic new capital measurements, and Production Theory in Economics*, (Michigan: ProQuest LLC, 2010) and,
https://order.proquest.com/OA_HTML/pqdtibeCCtpItmDspRte.jsp

Books web page at,
http://bahfecon.wix.com/bahfecon

- *Teconomics of Verbalism*, Utah FERDAT Publishing 2012, and at,
https://www.createspace.com/4121720,
   Books web page at,
http://bahfecon.wix.com/bahfecon

- *Analytical Remedies for The Millennial Cascading Economic Declines,* Utah FERDAT Publishing 2012, and at,
https://www.createspace.com/4187823,

- "The Demand and Supply Sides of Appropriate Technological Advancement." (Research paper at University of Utah Economics Dept. 2003),

- "Economic Theories and Practices in Technological Changes, capital measures, and Production." (Research paper at University of Utah Economics Dept. 1988).
- Fakhraie, Bahman, "The Demand and Supply Sides of Appropriate Technological Advancement." (Research paper at University of Utah Economics Dept. 2003).
- "Hallowing headless nations? The need to invest on public education under the 1980s international economic conditions," (Research paper at University of Utah Economics Dept. 1988).
- "Transfer of Technologies and Socioeconomic Theories of Dualism," (Research paper at University of Utah Economics Dept. 1983).

Production theory in Agriculture
Agro-production, Sheep production in Iran (an onsite research project 1975)
Monetary Macroeconomic Specialization (Milton Freedman,)
International Monetary macroeconomic Specializations (Robert Mundell)
Fiscal Analysis of oscillatory modifications
Applied Agricultural production in developing economies
Inappropriate Technology Transfers by Corporations and dualistic induced instabilities in a pre-democratic economies.
Certificate in Rural Development from Utah State University
Research Skills:
Statistical packages, data selection, analysis, and formulations.
Computer Languages, Spread Sheet Data Analysis, Writings
Multimedia & Creative Skills: Film and video production, CD: audio and video works
Languages: Fluent in English and Farsi, I can read and write some French, and Arabic.
              Fluent in Dezfili Dari dialectic [One of the earliest spoken languages]
Teaching Experiences:
University of Utah: macroeconomic and microeconomic: introductory course, and related mathematics.
Utah State University: Economic Department, Persian language, and cultural studies to faculty and students, and teaching assistance for Agricultural economics.
Volunteer Helping of other students
Student leadership positions AUSU, as an undergraduate
PROFESSIONAL EXPERIENCE:

Founder and Management of Money Wise Firm (A Private Financial Education Foundation for Personal Financial studies), 1970 to date
Volunteer work: President; V.P., and Treasurer of Cherrywood Association Inc., multimillion dollars project, (Different 3 year cycles 1980 to 1999, consultation to date)
Real Estate Investor and Renovations, General Manger, to date
Agribusiness management, owner manager
Auto Agency sale manager/sold
Auto shop management/sold
Numerous Volunteer Projects: planning, budgeting, contracting, and finishing.
Beside educational publications, and digital multi-media CDS, DVD formats, copyrighted at USA the library of congress.

Other Experience:
Budget Analysis, Budget Setting, Budget Forecasting, Asset Allocation Studies, Portfolio Analysis Studies, Saving (Goal Setting) Plan, Tax Management Studies, Risk/Reward Management and studies, Economic Condition risk Analysis, Managerial Goal Setting and Project Production Process and Enactments.
Economic Topics of Research and Lectures:
 Non-Marxist Revolutions in Middle East (Iran)
 Economic and Indices (Measurement Issues)
 Economic Theories of Technological Changes and Capital Measures
 Technological Change, Growth Rate, and Capital Formations with US Data
 Education and Taxation
 Hollowing Headless Nations! Education Crisis
 Technological Parameters Statistical Measurements
 New Econometric Measurements of Capital in Production Theory

Reading (Economic, Science, Mathematics, Econometrics, Statistics, Mystery, Ancients), Films (art, industry), Jazz, Foreign Eclectics music, Fly-fishing

BOOK PROMOTIONS

Techonological Injection, Dynamic New Capital measirements, and Production Theory in Economics

The New Scientific and Economic Foundations and New Production Theory Variables for the Modern Millennial Wealth Creation

Dr. Bahman Fakhraie's books web page link,
http://bahfecon.wix.com/bahfecon

DEMAND & SUPPLY SIDES OF TECHNOLOGICAL INJECTIONS

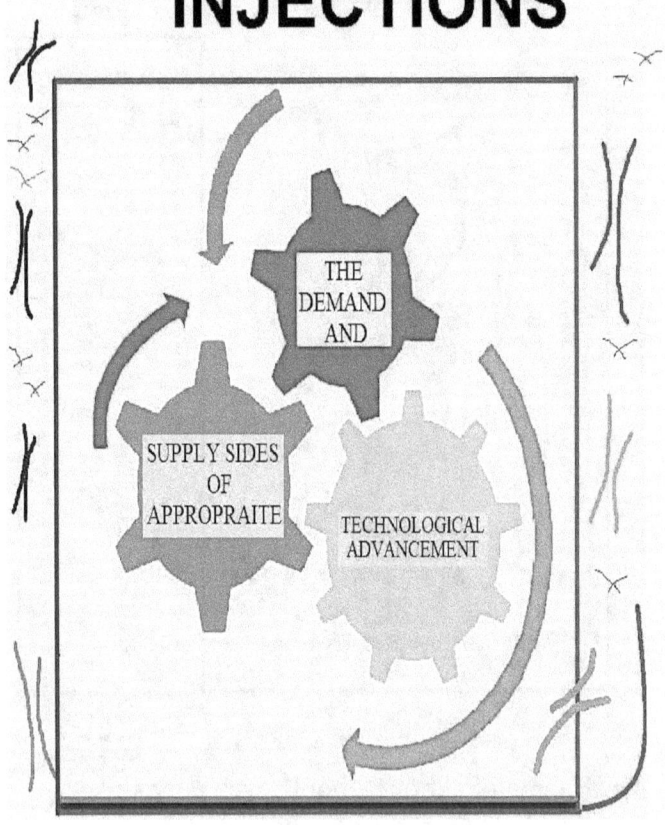

Dr. Bahman Fakhraie's books web page link,
http://bahfecon.wix.com/bahfecon

Book link, *https://www.createspace.com/4187823*

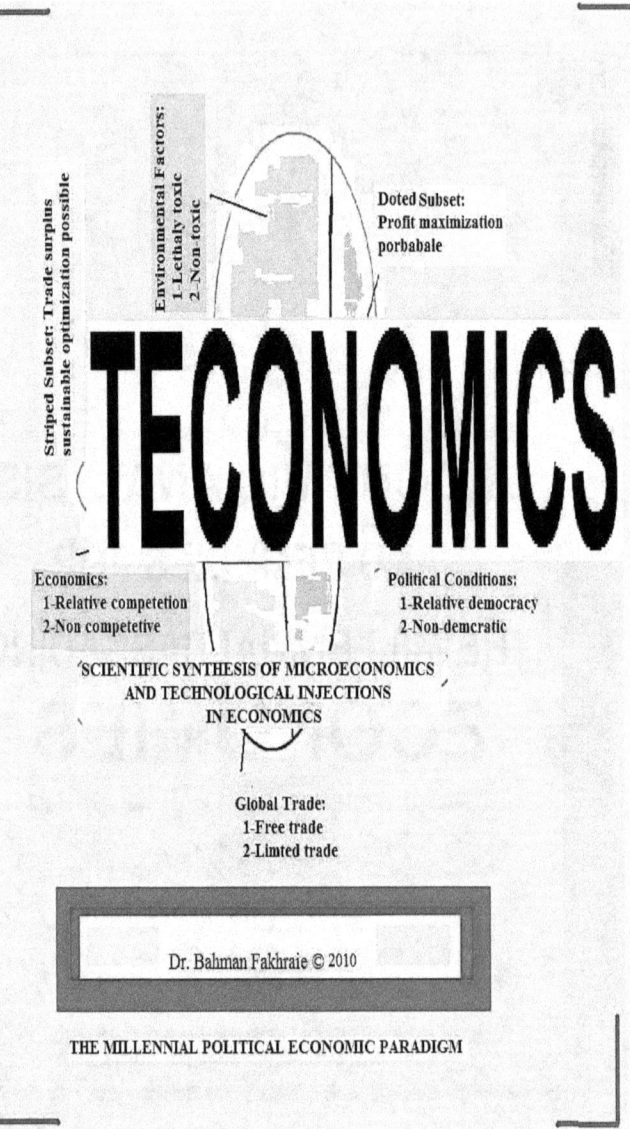

Book link, *https://www.createspace.com/4196760*

TECONOMICS OF VERBALISM

Bahman Fakhraie, Ph.D.

https://www.createspace.com/4121720

TECONOMICS
OF
DYNAMIC SUSTAINABLE
BUDGETS

Dynamic Sustainable Modular Production Budgets

Bahman Fakhraie, Ph.D.

https://www.createspace.com/4536462?ref=1147694&utm_id=6026

TREATISE ON TECONOMICS ØF

DYNAMIC RISKS

ALL NATURAL DISASTERS,  & ENERGY RESOURCES PRODCUTION DISASTERS

Bahman Fakhraie, Ph.D.

https://www.createspace.com/4187823

EBook, http://www.amazon.com/POLITICAL-MONOPOLISTIC-CAPITALISM-WEALTH-CONCENTRATION-ebook/dp/B00HQPBZBK/ref=sr_1_1/180-8302534-5503723?s=digital-text&ie=UTF8&qid=1389203920&sr=1-1#reader_B00HQPBZBK
Print Books link, *http://bahfecon.wix.com/bahfecon*

Dr. Bahman Fakhraie's books,
http://bahfecon.wix.com/bahfecon

To All Lives

Dr. Bahman Fakhraie, PhD in Economics, University of Utah, and his dissertation added to the influences of the Unorthodox Holistic Economic doctrine and complemented the modern orthodox economic theories, in the millennial age of technological paradigm shifts. He applies analytical skills with gestalt study of history, mathematics, and econometrics to economic analysis, with scientific background. He is a Published Economist, Author, Researcher, Investor, and Private Contractor. His skills are in international trade and finance, economic production (theory and application), growth and development theory, econometrics, agriculture economics, and agronomy. These are greatly valued skills combinations to employ. Books links, http://bahfecon.wix.com/bahfecon

ISBN-10:0989453995
ISBN-13:978-0-9894539-9-8
Library of Congress copyright
Case Number, 11156931041

www.ingramcontent.com/pod-product-compliance
Lightning Source LLC
Chambersburg PA
CBHW070643300426
44111CB00013B/2243